George N. Cahill: Backward Glances

Michael J. Cahill

Published by Mary Luisa Press, 2022.

GEORGE N. CAHILL: BACKWARD GLANCES

First edition. August 19, 2022.

Copyright © 2022 Michael J. Cahill.

ISBN: 979-8201730604

Written by Michael J. Cahill.

Table of Contents

For my father, whose great good humor, moral decency and simple kindness continue to outdistance the life he's lived.

Origins

When my father was 88 my mother, his darling wife of 62 years, was lost to our family through sudden illness. It devastated us all. After her death there was every reason for a man of his devotion to recede into grief. Instead he chose to stretch his resolve and reach more deeply into the lives of his children and grandchildren. Seven months later my father and I were on a journey up the west coast from Los Angeles to Vancouver to see a home from my childhood, driving into our future by visiting our past.

That was eleven years ago and it turned out to be a bittersweet beginning to an ongoing journey of discovery. The world from which he had evolved was a distant, mysterious place to me, one I'd only ever caught glimpses of growing up. For most of my life I'd understood little of my father's history; the finer details of his youth, his education, or any of the events that shaped his upbringing. As children we all knew some of the basics but few of the circumstances. Ongoing conversations with him over the past few years have cast him in an entirely new light for me. As he finishes navigating his 100th year, I am still discovering new things about this man I've known all my life. At the same time I've learned how very little I understood of the context that always made him marvelous to me.

Of my father's father, George Newton Cahill Sr., and of his grandfather, Thomas Joseph Cahill who emigrated from Ireland to America, precious few records exist. Chapter One is the result of what little my research could bear, though it's nowhere near as detailed as one would wish.

As for my father's own story, the following chronology began as an idle query about his earliest recollections and, like a boulder tipping loose from a mountain top, the questioning continued, building a momentum all its own. I had to write it all down or these charming, tragic, touching scraps of his life might otherwise be lost to me.

Along the way I'd mention some new revelation to one of my brothers or sisters, to which they'd often respond that Dad or Mom had told them the same story years before. And thus it became more clear that parents share different things with different children and that there can never be an equity of information for all.

While some events here may be familiar to the family, others will be new and, hopefully, many more have yet to be added by those with better recall than my father's and my own. At best this is an assembly of snapshots, many out of focus. I don't pretend this story is in any way comprehensive, and for any errors of fact, date or detail, I alone am responsible.

My parents were no world beaters. But neither were they idle with their time because, in their marriage and careers, they crafted a gentle and loving adventure very much worth preserving. Do I kick myself for not having thought to do this 20 years ago when this story was younger and my mother was here to add to its richness? I do. Mom had a particularly wonderful mind for minutiae and effortlessly recalled names, dates, locations and events replete with all their attendant personality, color and detail.

My father, while not as strong on the smaller specifics, nonetheless possessed a firm embrace of the broader picture and had a great heart for just how much those magnificent life moments were felt — a heart, it turns out, that had been roomier and more romantic than any of us might have ever imagined.

Allowing me to interview him and to trespass among his memories has been one of the greatest joys I think I will know in this life.

M.J.C.
Summer 2022

1

The Man from Thurles

George Cahill Jr.'s grandfather is said to have been born December 1st 1863 as Thomas Joseph Cahill in Thurles (pronounced DUR-las), County Tipperary, in the south of Ireland on the banks of the River Suir. Little is known of Thomas or his family during his upbringing other than he was born on the long heels of Ireland's great potato famine (1845-1847) which destroyed practically every potato crop in the land with black mold, making the country's predominant food source inedible.

Between 1845 and 1855, during the crisis years of the famine and its immediate aftermath, the country's population of 8.2 million shrank by a third. Starvation and disease killed 1.1 million and emigration claimed another 2 million. At the end of the famine, one out of every three people in Ireland was gone. Those who tried to escape the country's devastating pestilence found passage on mostly merchant vessels, many of which would come to be known as the famine ships.

Prior to 1855 during the height of the potato famine exodus, merchant vessels conveying Irish immigrants in steerage class were commonly referred to as "coffin ships". Record numbers of 19th-century immigrants arrived in American port cities from Western Europe — but that's only if they managed to survive the journey. Many of the new arrivals were desperately poor, paid very little for their passage, and were treated as nothing more than cargo by shipping companies.

One of the United States' first immigration laws, the Steerage Act, passed on March 2, 1819, was a half-hearted attempt to improve such transatlantic travel conditions. But the regulations it introduced did little to address the horrors of 19th-century travel in Steerage (a catch-all term for the lowest class of sea travel). In 1847 alone, close to 5,000 people died from diseases like typhus and dysentery on ships bound for America.

Disease thrived in the squalid conditions of steerage travel, where, depending on the size of a ship, a few hundred to 1,000 people could be crammed into tight quarters. Wooden beds, known as berths, were stacked two- to three-high with two people sharing single berths, and up to four squeezed into a double. The only ventilation was provided by hatches to the upper decks, which were locked tight during rough seas and storms.

Since the only bathrooms were located above deck, passengers trapped below during stormy weather were forced to urinate, defecate (and get seasick) in buckets, which would overturn in the churning waves. The stench was unbearable and deadly diseases like typhoid, cholera and smallpox spread unabated.

Food was also in constant shortage. Some ships required passengers to bring their own meager provisions, while others provided only minimum rations meant to keep passengers from starving. A lack of clean drinking water and rancid food resulted in rampant bouts of dysentery.

The U.S. Congress professed to respond to these inhumane conditions with the Steerage Act, which was supposed to set minimum standards for cross-Atlantic travel. The act imposed a stiff penalty for each passenger in excess of two people for every five tons of ship weight. It also laid down minimum provisions — 60 gallons of water and 100 pounds of "wholesome ship bread" per passenger — but only required those rations for ships leaving the U.S. ports for Europe, not immigrant vessels arriving in America.

The crux of the Steerage Act had been a new requirement that all arriving ships provide U.S. customs agents with a written manifest of everyone on board; their age, sex and occupation, their country of origin and final destination. Captains also had to report the number of names of all people who died during the voyage.

These customs records were the first to track the national origin of immigrants and would later lead to quotas (and bans) of certain ethnic groups, such as the Chinese Exclusion Act.

The light-handed regulations of the Steerage Act left the door open for so-called "coffin ships" or "famine ships" of the late 1840's that carried untold thousands of Irish citizens fleeing the Potato Famine. According to University of Nevada research, the average mortality rate of Irish coffin ships that made the fateful trip from Ireland to Quebec in 1847 was around 10 percent, and that at least two ships lost more than half their passengers.

While it's true that some Irish emigrants were already on the brink of death when they boarded the coffin ships, it's also true that tighter regulations and basic safeguards could have saved many lives. It wasn't until the mid 1850's that the U.S. Congress passed far more comprehensive regulations for passenger vessels. The Carriage of Passengers Act of 1855 specified the maximum number of steerage passengers per square feet of "clear space" (one person for every 18 square feet), listed detailed provisions that must be stocked for every ship, even those arriving in America, and most importantly, required ventilators to "carry off foul air" from the stifling steerage hold.

All decks and passenger compartments needed to be constructed in such a way as to allow for regular swabbing and disinfecting. In addition, a physician and "hospital" were required on board each ship. The law called for at least one bathroom per 100 passengers. And to help ensure compliance, the law stated that captains would be fined $10.00 ($200.00 today) for every passenger who died "by natural disease" during the voyage.

By 1855, though, the Great Famine was over and so was the typhoid scare. Mortality rates had already dropped significantly and the advent of the steamship had significantly reduced what had been a six-week transatlantic journey down to a much more accommodating 10-to-12 days. That's not to say steerage travel was a pleasant experience for the second half of the 19th century.

In 1879, when a journalist traveling from New York to Liverpool first stepped into the steerage compartment, he wrote[1], "Words are incapable of conveying anything like a correct notion of the kind of den in which I stood among 60 fellow passengers... The stench, combined with the heat, was simply intolerable."

Another writer, taking the reverse journey from Liverpool to New York in 1888, described the food served in steerage as barely edible, and then only when respite from seasickness allowed one to eat. Steerage passengers were required to bring their own cutlery and dishes and washing up was equally nauseating.

"The galley cook filled a tub with hot water on the less deck close by the rail," she wrote. "About this we stood in circles six deep waiting for a chance to rinse our platters. When my turn arrived the water was cold and diversified with archipelagoes of potato and meat. To be first at the tub, to wash my dishes while the water was clean, became the aspiration of my existence."

It would take Ireland many generations to regain any sense of prosperity. Thomas Cahill's birth in 1863 came at the beginning of that uphill climb and his parents were quite likely struggling along with their fellow countrymen in those desperate years following the famine. For whatever reason — be it destitution, lack of prospects, or perhaps even a sense of adventure — in April of 1883 19-year-old Thomas boarded a merchant steamer of Montreal registry called the *S.S. Nova Scotian* bound for America.

---

1.   https://www.gjenvick.com/Steerage/1879-SteerageAccommodations-Cunard.html

The ship's manifest listed his profession as "farmer", which may well be a clue to where he grew up and what his family did. Even though he would be turning 20 in December of that year, the passenger list recorded his age as 21, so either Thomas lied about his age or this entry was a misprint.

Birth certificates were not mandated in Ireland until 1864. Prior to that, all births, marriages and deaths were commonly entered into the church registry of the local parish. At the time, many births and deaths took place at home and were thus registered as soon as possible (sometimes within days or weeks) after the event. Since there does not appear to be a birth certificate for Thomas Cahill, and because a search of parish records from Thurles have yet to reveal a birth in his name, there also remains the remote possibility that he could well have been born in 1861, instead of 1863 (as his certificate of death states). Another possibility is that Thurles might have been his home but not his place of birth. Whatever the case, the surname "Cahill" was also an extremely common name at the time in Ireland, as were "Thomas" and "Joseph" so, though a few discovered documents have almost hit the mark, nothing conclusive has surfaced as of this writing. Absent any definitive documentation from Thurles, we have only Thomas Cahill's death certificate to go by to mark his birth.

The *Nova Scotian's* manifest denotes that there were, in addition to Thomas, 749 other passengers on board, most all of them in steerage. Their ages averaged between late teens and early 20's. Though the famine was long over, its devastating effects yet lingered and the youth of Ireland continued to flee their homeland. Professions among those aboard were predominantly listed as laborers, farmers, carpenters and domestics. The manifest records that only a few passengers checked luggage in the hold, but not Thomas, who presumably made the journey only with what he carried.

The *Nova Scotian* departed from Liverpool, England sometime in late March or early April of 1883 and made a stop at Queenstown,

Ireland to board its final passengers, including Thomas Cahill, before heading out across the great Atlantic. Though the port's original name was Cobh (pronounced COVE), in 1849 the British renamed the city Queenstown in honor of a visit from Queen Victoria. However, during the War of Irish Independence in 1920, the city took back its original name and today Cobh remains the country's largest deep water port on the southernmost tip of County Cork.

The *Nova Scotian* landed in Boston, Massachusetts May 14th 1883. At the time both Boston and New York were the primary points of entry for 19th century immigrants. Ellis Island would not be in operation as a point of immigration until 1890. By the late 1800's nativism had peaked and become a general term of opposition to immigration based on fears that, according to opposition groups of the time, immigrants will "distort or spoil" existing cultural values. *"In situations where immigrants greatly outnumber the original inhabitants, nativist movements seek to prevent cultural change."*

Such were the circumstances in 1894 when three former Harvard law school classmates established one such group, the Immigration Restriction League[2]. The aim of the organization was "exclusion of elements undesirable" from the country.

Nativism took a considerable toll and, among the many discriminations suffered by international newcomers, one of the most common in Boston was a sign displayed in the windows of businesses seeking employees.

It read <u>NINA</u> — No Irish Need Apply.

Despite the city's already considerable Irish population, Boston did not hold Thomas Cahill. His first few years in America are not well recorded, however at some point he migrated to Washington, D.C. where his family is listed on a census form dated June 10, 1890. Here

---

2.   https://www.thecrimson.com/article/2018/10/18/immigration-restriction-league/

his residence is noted as 1620 14th Street, Washington, D.C. His age on his next birthday is recorded as 27 and his profession is listed as that of "clerk in a tea store".

The form also states his wife is Blanche R. Cahill age 23, and daughter is Bessie R. Cahill age 1. Interestingly, in the space asking "Number of Years in the United States" Thomas answered "5", even though he would have been in America just over seven years at this point.

About six weeks after this census form was filed, Blanche gave birth to their second child Helen Marie Cahill on August 21st 1890. Five years later Thomas' first son Edmund Albert Cahill was born.

During their time in Washington, Thomas became good friends with Newton D. Baker who was a geologist and law student. Born December 3rd 1871, Baker was eight years and two days younger than Thomas. They knew each other while Newton attended and then graduated from Law School. Baker then left in June of 1897. He moved to Cleveland, Ohio where he built up a successful law career and got into politics, eventually becoming Mayor of Cleveland in 1911.

Thomas' friend Newton was doing well.

At age 33 Thomas Cahill moved his family to Jacksonville, Florida where he became manager of the city's very first Great Atlantic and Pacific Tea Company store, part of a chain of stores that would shortly evolve into the A&P grocery store conglomerate.

Blanche was known for using pampas grass for interior decorating, as well as being an enthusiastic collector of Octagon Soap coupons which could be redeemed for gifts from the Octagon catalogue. She kept a drawer full of these coupons, all fastidiously organized, plotting the many goods that could be acquired with enough of them. The house was almost completely furnished with lamps, dishes, linens and appliances, even clothing, and all delivered courtesy of the Octagon Soap catalogue.

Blanche was also adamant that her hair be washed only in rainwater. She even had a special tank installed at the back of the house to catch runoff from the roof whenever it rained, which was often.

Having grown up in Washington, DC, she had a deep-rooted, diehard relationship with her hometown team. She'd always been a voracious consumer of baseball and, even after relocating to Florida, whenever her beloved Washington Senators were playing, Blanche was riveted to the radio, and woe be to anyone who distracted her from the game. She knew all the players' names, numbers, positions and averages. She was an astute aficionado of the game, a great scorekeeper, and her enthusiasm for the Senators knew no bounds.

On March 10th 1898 Blanche and Thomas produced a second son, George Newton Cahill — whose middle name was bestowed in honor of Thomas' friend Newton D. Baker.

Interestingly, in 1916 President Woodrow Wilson named Newton Baker as Secretary of War for the United States where he presided over the United States Army through 1917 and 1918 for the remainder of the war.

The 1897 Jacksonville city directory listed the Great A&P Tea Company's address as 11 West Bay Street. But on May 3rd 1901 an historically devastating fire burned the majority of downtown Jacksonville to the ground — including Thomas' store. Martial law was declared in the city and a photograph taken three days after the fire on a corner close to where his store once stood shows nothing but a pile of smoldering rubble. 7 people died, 10,000 were left homeless, and it remains the third most destructive fire of a city in U.S. history (after the devastating San Francisco fire spawned by the 1906 earthquake, and the Great Chicago fire of 1871).

One has to wonder what action, if any, that Thomas may have taken on that fateful Friday afternoon in May of 1901 to try to save his store. The fire tore through downtown Jacksonville and the A&P store was on one of the last blocks to burn, some eight hours after the fire started. This fire also destroyed the Duval County Courthouse including almost a century's worth of public records such as licenses, along with birth, marriage and death certificates. This may well explain why research turned up so few relevant Cahill records.

The Great A&P Tea Company was rebuilt next door to its prior site. The 1904 city directory still lists Thomas Cahill as the store's manager but at the new address (just 25 feet west of the old location) now at 13 W. Bay Street. Unfortunately the store no longer exists, nor any of its neighboring Jacksonville businesses, as the entire city block is now a multi-level parking structure supporting a massive shopping complex directly across the street to the south.

Early on, Thomas and Blanche had a house at 30 West 4th Street just a few miles north of his store in Jacksonville. As of this writing the house still stands and remains a private residence.

Some time after the great 1901 fire, the Cahills purchased a home at 343 West 26th St. in Jacksonville. This house also remains today.

On September 26, 1905 a third daughter arrived named Dorothy Burbridge Cahill ("Burb"), and on the 5th of July 1911 Blanche gave birth to their third son and sixth child Thomas Patrick Cahill.

Sadly, when Thomas senior was 55, his first son Edmund, died at the age of 23, a victim of the 1918 influenza pandemic.

There are no records indicating how long Thomas continued to manage the A&P store on West Bay St. in Jacksonville. In later years he is shown to have taken various jobs, mostly as a guard or watchman, including as a Special Agent for the Atlantic Coast Line (ACL) Railroad.

His death certificate indicates that cirrhosis of the liver was evident and that a possible heart condition may have contributed his death. He passed away on September 28th 1928.

He was 64.

His wife Blanche would survive him another 22 years and continued to live in the house on 26th St. Her daughter Helen and sons George and Thomas also lived with her there for a time after Thomas' death. Blanche remained in the house until all her children left. She then moved in with her daughter Elizabeth ("Bessie") who had purchased a home in the Jacksonville suburb of Lake Forest. She lived with Bessie until she passed away in 1950 at the age of 82. Blanche Cahill had outlived two of her six children.

Thomas and Blanche's fourth child George Newton Cahill Sr. spent most of his life in Jacksonville, Florida. He was 29 when he lost his father, Thomas, who passed away just a few months shy of his 65th birthday (and one year prior to the start of the Great Depression).

Thomas Joseph Cahill had lived to see his second son marry and pass on the family name to a grandson.

George Newton Cahill Jr. turned 6-years-old just three weeks before his Irish grandfather died.

2

A Modern Family

In 1915 George Newton Cahill Sr., a lanky, energetic and personable young man, was working across the street from a Jacksonville millinery where Mae Iverine Hettrick was employed. The happy fellow regularly waved hello to Mae and eventually introduced himself and asked her out. Mae and George were married August 28, 1916 and lived in his mother's house.

The next year their first child Margaret Cahill was born. Sadly, Margaret died of unknown causes when she was only three weeks old.

George and Mae picked themselves up and their second child, another daughter, Carolyn Bernice, was born the following year on August 31st in the midst of the 1918 influenza pandemic when Mae was 22. Their next daughter Mary Catherine arrived two years later on December 14, 1920.

Then when she was 26, Mae Cahill went into labor yet again, this time on a Sunday afternoon, and George Newton Cahill Jr. arrived in the world mere minutes into Monday on September 5th 1922. George Jr. was the first boy in a family of two older girls. One last bundle of joy arrived in their midst when little sister Elizabeth Ann ("Betty") was born on the 6th of April 1927.

Life moved along uneventfully for the six Cahills throughout much of the 1920's and, while George's happy family was by no means well off, neither were they struggling to get by. That began to change for them, and for the rest of the country, in a matter of days following young George's 7th birthday.

After the great New York stock market crash of 1929, the domino effect of Wall Street's collapse rippled well into the nation's heartland

and left no family untouched. People who'd been comfortable were suddenly struggling and those who'd been struggling were suddenly poor. Unable to meet payrolls, giant corporations executed massive layoffs, medium sized companies began to fold, and far too many small businesses shuttered their doors. Americans were unemployed by the millions, families lost their homes, and lines at soup kitchens ran for blocks and blocks. America had never seen such personal devastation. The most representative song of the era was *"Brother, Can You Spare a Dime?"*

As though the country suddenly finding itself in the throes of a major depression wasn't trouble enough, one Sunday when he was about eight years old, George Jr. was riding between his mother and his father in the front seat of their car. They came to a stop at a railroad crossing to wait for a train. Once it had passed and traffic started moving, their car quickly got up to speed, only to have the vehicle in front of them stop abruptly. Not noticing until the last moment, George Sr. hit the brakes hard. They avoided hitting the other car but the sudden stop threw young George into the windshield, shattering it. While drawing his head back into the car his little face caught a large piece of jagged glass hanging down from the window frame, severing almost completely the lower half of his nose and leaving it suspended by only a small tract of skin.

A woman in the car behind them was a nurse and, seeing the incident, ran up to help. She immediately took control and gently eased the detached element back where it belonged saying, "Here, little boy, hold the end in place against the rest of your nose. We'll take you to the hospital, they'll sew it back on for you and it won't ever be a problem." Her calm and measured manner steadied everyone's nerves.

To the hospital they all went and, just as the woman predicted, a delicate surgery did the trick. The scar from that accident lingered for another six years or so, after which it all but disappeared. Whenever George would tell this story in years to come, a brief examination of a spot just below the bridge of his nose betrayed a telltale remnant of that scar. Otherwise, one would never suspect it had ever happened.

A federal mandate for safety glass in cars would not be enacted until 1937.

The economy was slow to improve and by 1931 the depression had taken such a grim toll that George Sr.'s long time employer the Groover-Stewart Drug Company in Jacksonville was finally forced to pare down its ranks. During a brief stint in the U.S. Navy in 1918, George Sr. had served as a pharmacist's mate, the training for which he parlayed into a profession after the war. But now, after 12 years as a pharmacist technician for Groover-Stewart, he was suddenly out of a job and, with a wife and four kids to support, George's options quickly evaporated. With no small sense of regret, he conceded to an offer from a thousand miles away.

Mae's brothers Vernon and Wilmer Hettrick operated a coal yard in Detroit and, since practically all homes and businesses in the north were dependent on coal burning furnaces, there was a booming business in coal.

Having been a Florida boy all his life, George Sr. was not well suited for Michigan's bracing winters. Nonetheless the family made the difficult trek north where they were invited to share a good sized house with Mae's brother Vernon, his wife Pauline and their two children. Radical adjustments would be expected of everyone. George and Mae had their own room, the three girls shared another room, and George Jr. slept on a cot.

About the time they arrived in Detroit many black families had also migrated north to find work, the backlash from which resulted in a number of ugly race riots throughout the early 1930s. Mae and George were disgusted by the racism and its attendant violence. So many people were brutalized and killed in the riots that it jarred the couple's sense of what life in the north was going to be like.

Whether in response to the desperate circumstance of a nationwide depression, or of having to share her house with six extra people — or even perhaps just owing to her own natural disposition — Uncle Vernon's wife was not the easiest person to live with. Young George and his sisters disliked Pauline Hettrick greatly and with justification.

"She was mean", recalled George Jr.

From the moment the Cahills landed in Detroit, every aspect of Pauline's behavior was that of disdain. They were treated by her as poor relatives. Not so much through direct action, but rather by mood and manner, it was regularly made clear the Cahills were not welcome.

The Hettrick brothers' coal business was strenuous work. They would load raw coal into 50-pound sacks, hoist them high onto trucks and make deliveries. At each house or business the sacks were hefted to an outside hatch and manually emptied down a chute into a basement where the occupants would use the supply to fuel their furnaces.

Every day when George and his brothers-in-law returned home they were weary, drained, and quite literally pitch black from head to toe with coal dust and soot ground into every pore. From the very first George Sr. hated the back breaking work. He hated the inescapable grime of coal, hated the monotony of the job, hated the cold, hated everything about Detroit. Demoralized, drained and with no funds to spare, George Sr.'s evenings and weekends were devoured by his exhaustion. No more wrestling matches, dances or ball games — all the delightful pastimes that had happily filled the family's leisure hours in Florida.

And no more singing.

George Jr. remembered his father having a marvelous singing voice which had served him well in his youth as a one-time member of a Florida Vaudeville company. Before the family's move to Detroit, George Sr. used to sing all the time, a happy-go-lucky sort of singing, to himself, to his children, or just chiming in with any old song on the Victrola or radio, a clear, throaty, confident crooner. But Detroit had now robbed him of that once-jovial mood. His children were immediately struck by the difference in his composure, yet they understood all too well his plight.

In the daytime Mae had a job making women's hats, a skill she'd acquired at the millinery in Jacksonville where she and George first met. At night she worked as a taxi-dancer. Taxi-dance halls gained popularity in the 1920's and 30's where men could hire women to dance with them for a sum of money. Ballroom dancing had previously been a pastime reserved for the elite, but in this new style of dance parlor, working class people began twirling around the room as well.

Taxi-dance halls had little in common with the stuffy ballroom affairs favored by the upper classes. Rather, they were informal and boisterous. A typical patron, upon entry, would exchange a dollar for a strip of ten tickets, each one good for a dance. The women were more commonly known as dime-a-dance girls, but also as taxi-dancers because their pay was proportional to the amount of time they would spend dancing with a customer as would a cab driver spend with a passenger. Taxi-dancing attracted a diverse crowd of entertainment goers that previously had neither the access nor the ability to dance with women at a ballroom. To labor all day hunched over a table making hats and then spend her evenings smiling and dancing non-stop with strangers left Mae exhausted as well.

Though he never so much declared to them how he despised the situation, George's children deduced their father's misery from his general demeanor and from conversations overheard between their parents. Despite a lifelong penchant for healthy athletic endeavor, the coal yard was taking an awful physical toll on George. He toughed it out for almost a year until he could endure no more and ultimately declared Florida was where they belonged.

The Great Depression was in full grind with people in the city unemployed by the tens of thousands. Meeting the needs of a full household on their pooled meager incomes was challenge enough. But, while neither of her jobs were easy, Mae felt the south offered no better opportunities. She was determined to stick it out in Detroit and she and George finally agreed to an amicable divorce. He would return to the more temperate climate of Florida and the kind of "clean" work for which he felt better suited. The pact they made was that Mae would keep the children with her. Then every summer, during the two or so months that the kids were out of school, they would spend that time with their father in Florida. George kissed his children goodbye and promptly unshackled himself from Detroit, never to return.

Though young George only saw his dad in the summer months when they went to stay with him, there was never really any oppressive sense of missing his father. The two had a firm, comradely relationship which would only grow deeper in later years. For the time being each knew his place and life in Detroit for young George was filled with school and jobs and music.

And reading.

Once when a prolonged illness left George Jr. bedridden for two weeks, his uncle Wilmer showed up with a great box of old books. To pass the time George started poring over these adventurous volumes, including several boys series like The Rover Boys and The Hardy Boys, Tarzan and Tom Swift. George quickly discovered he loved to read. He burned through everything in Uncle Wilmer's box and was hooked. Encouraged by a teacher, he even joined a book club at school. He spent a good deal of time at the school's well stocked library, as well as the public library, trucking home numerous volumes every month.

Each night around 9:00, just before bed, George would fix himself a bowl of Corn Flakes. He loved Corn Flakes. They often couldn't afford fresh milk so he mixed caramel-colored condensed milk from a can with water to pour on the cereal. While he ate his bedtime snack he would read. Whatever was available. A newly borrowed book, an old newspaper or even the side of the cereal box. Anything that happened to be lying around. It was an addiction.

In years to come, many of his own children's most enduring memories of him would be of his weekly treks to the library, returning home with armloads of books, and evenings spent in his favorite arm chair immersed in a spy novel or the latest technical thriller.

George Jr. was a keen observer of his mother's hardships and didn't want to impose on her for the things a young boy craves. His parents' sturdy work ethic had emboldened him. Early on he found various jobs so he could earn his own money. He scrounged up any odd job like delivering flyers and advertisements for local businesses. One day when he and his mother were at a thrift market in which she knew the owner, the man blurted out, "George, we need some help here. You wanna job?" George signed on right away, stocking shelves and portioning out sugar, flour and potatoes from large shipping sacks into smaller bags for easy sale. He also made deliveries for customers who were unable to carry home larger orders.

On one occasion while hurrying to cross a street with a delivery, the wagon he was using to pull the groceries overturned on some tracks, which in turn caused an approaching streetcar to have to stop and wait. He recalled the humiliation of people laughing while he struggled to upright the wagon and reload it so the passenger-filled car could continue on its way. Two men actually dismounted the streetcar to help him reload the wagon. For some years after, this awkward incident would echo as an early embarrassment.

As an adolescent, there was never a time when George didn't have a job. Working early on and making his own money meant he didn't have to trouble his mother for extras. And working allowed him to invest in one of his greatest passions — music. He adored the sounds of Benny Goodman, Glenn Miller, Paul Whiteman, and Jimmy and Tommy Dorsey. Big bands were all the rage in the 30's and 40's and the radio just couldn't play enough of his favorites. He judiciously filled out his extensive record collection, earnestly assembled with his own money and made up primarily of all the big bands.

In the winter of 1932, back in his beloved Jacksonville, George Sr. moved into his parents' house at 343 West 26th Street shared by his mother Blanche and his brother Thomas. Cashing in once again on his pharmacy credentials, George Sr. took a job as a clerk at Raymond H. Carswell Drugs at 3301 Main Street, and as a part time tax collector. In January of '33 he landed a full time job with the Duvall County Tax Collector's Office in the Jacksonville courthouse where he would spend the next 15 years, eventually working his way up to Chief Deputy in charge of Occupational Licenses. He was happy to once again make a respectable wage and regain his old vitality. In fact he became so fit he was signed to play semi-pro baseball with the Jacksonville City League, in addition to running marathons and entering track events with the YMCA. At 34 years of age he was in the best shape of his life.

Summers in Jacksonville with his visiting children occasionally consisted of George Sr. renting a beach cottage for the season. He continued working throughout the summer, relying on a hired girl to watch Mary, Carolyn and George Jr. during the day. Betty was missed, of course, because neither her mother nor father could persuade her to join her siblings on their summer vacation. Carolyn and Mary could always entertain each other and, when he wasn't exploring or reading, young George managed to come up with his own distractions.

There wasn't a lot of trouble for him to get into, though one small instance of boyhood mischief presented itself as there happened to be an enclosed public shower stall with a locking door very close to the cottage they had leased that summer. Beach bathers used it to change into and out of their swim suits and rinse off the salt water. Interestingly the shower had no roof. And the upper sun deck of the rental cottage offered a strategic vantage point for any enterprising adolescent who cared to lean out at just the right angle to exercise a perfectly innocent youthful curiosity. On one occasion in particular an attractive teenage girl caught George in mid observation and gave him what for at quite a pique of fit.

According to George, his father was, far and away the most well liked man he ever knew. Young George recalled the many, many times he walked or rode with his father through downtown Jacksonville and George Sr. would repeatedly be met with the heartiest of greetings from every passer by — men, women, children, shop workers, police, pedestrians and drivers of every stripe calling out with brightest enthusiasm, "Hey, George!", "How ya doin', George?!", "Great to see ya, George!" and so on.

How could one man possibly be so beloved?

It was not only a tribute to his father's forthright personality and jocular manner. It was also quite something for a young boy to see his dad so dearly and widely admired by almost every person in town, which only served to redouble his already considerable affection for the man. What it boiled down to was that George Sr. possessed a lively knack for close friendships and seemed in every way to be the practical embodiment of Will Rogers' famous claim: "I never met a man I didn't like."

Just after he was promoted in the tax office to handing out business licenses, he was approached by a young black man who'd been trying for a couple of years to acquire a license to open his own cleaning establishment but had repeatedly been refused for no clear reason. George Sr. promptly told the fellow, "Of course you qualify. Why wouldn't I give you a license?"

Thereafter young George recalled that whenever his father stopped in to pick up his dry cleaning, however earnestly he tried to pay, the eternally grateful shop owner simply wouldn't allow it. Never once.

While their father gave all the children equal time, George Jr. recalls most fondly the activities shared between just the two of them. George Sr., as a semi-pro ball player, was a pretty darned good one. Young George accompanied him to games and cheered from the stands while his dad played. He excelled as a pitcher and left fielder but was also a gifted switch hitter. Being ambidextrous at bat, he connected with the ball, either right- or left-handed, with equal agility. Depending on the pitcher, George Sr. could master any number of combinations fired from the mound and still rack up the runs. How can any kid not admire such devastating athleticism?

Favorite spectator events for father and son were professional wrestling and boxing. Jacksonville was a hot spot for sports, and droves of popular fighters competed in local bouts, almost all of whom seemed to know George Sr. personally. If he didn't know them he was quick to introduce himself and his boy, often times inviting the athletes back to the house for drinks and stories of life in the ring.

Young George recalled meeting a wide variety of regional and nationally known fighters, especially "Two Ton" Tony Galento, who later fought Joe Louis in his bid for the 1939 world heavyweight championship. The cigar chomping pugilist got his nickname when, once, coming from his day job, he was almost late for a fight and explained to his manager, "I had two tons of ice to deliver." Though he'd been built like a cement truck with a talent for knocking down giants, he was kind enough to pay attention to George Sr.'s little boy, who carried an autograph book and collected the signatures of every famous and almost famous fighter that came to town. The autograph book of course is now long gone. But the cherished memories of those many sports encounters shared with his father still loomed large some ninety years on.

During those summers when he couldn't afford a beach house, George Sr. boarded the kids at his sister's house next door to his mother's. The children got to spend quality time with their beloved aunt Bessie and grandmother Blanche, and with Uncle Tommy, George Sr.'s younger brother, who was widely regarded as a wild man.

Tommy Cahill spent years cultivating a reputation as something of a scoundrel. "He was the worst character you ever saw", George Jr. recalled with great fondness and "was known in the family for always doing the most outrageous things." He had been married and divorced "three or four times." Owing to his fear of dentists, Tommy had really terrible teeth. But he had the most beautiful handwriting of anyone George ever knew with "gorgeous, flowing cursive penmanship." A real artist of the written word.

In later years Tommy was not as favorably considered by his nieces, as they recalled him being dismissive of girls in the family. But with the boys, Uncle Tommy was remembered as being terribly generous with his time, spending a good deal of it with young George. One summer in particular George Jr. recalled that he and his cousin Frank Long were treated to a bout of spontaneous creativity. From a stand of bamboo trees that grew in his mother's back yard, Tommy harvested a stalk of bamboo, cut it to size and ingeniously fashioned two fully functional pop guns for the the boys. He did many such nice things for young George who always remembered his crazy, fun loving Uncle Tommy with great affection.

Back in Detroit with their father no longer around, Mae spent more time with the children than ever before, always talking to them. There was no money to go out to shows so she took the kids to parks and on picnics and told them stories, especially of when she was little. A favorite story involved one night when Mae was a girl. She recalled coming back from an outing with her family to find they'd locked themselves out. Mae volunteered to crawl in through her bedroom window. When she got to the front door to let everyone in, she pretended she'd been unable to see in the dark to find the pull string for the lights. Her mother stepped inside, eyes not yet adjusted to the dark, and instinctively reached for the string only to find Mae's hand already there. Thinking it an intruder lurking in the dark, the woman shrieked with fright. Mae found this very entertaining and recounted the prank to her own children with glee.

George Jr. recalls his mother being "very funny" and always ready for anything that made you laugh. Mae was not above playing little jokes on her own kids. In fact she relished every opportunity to demonstrate the art of having fun.

One day while cleaning out the refrigerator Mae discovered a plate of long neglected Jello that had grown a layer of fuzzy mold. Instead of relegating it to the garbage pail, she took the disgusting mass in hand and went to the basement door where she called downstairs to young George. When he arrived at the bottom of the stairs saying, "Yes, mam?", she replied, "Catch this." The startled boy shrieked when what could only have been a dead rat or other decomposing creature splattered into his hands. They both laughed and laughed.

Unfortunately her youngest daughter Betty had been saddled with an overactive bladder and every day after school, like clockwork, the poor girl would burst through the door at the exact same time, race to the bathroom and plant herself to have a pee. On one auspicious afternoon, just moments before Betty's big entrance, Mae gathered the other children to let them in on her conspiracy. This loving, considerate mother of four had minutes earlier slathered the toilet seat with a few dollops of peanut butter. Sure enough, here comes Betty, through the front door and sprinting down the hall. Within seconds of the bathroom door closing came a scream, an "EEEWWWW!" and more screams, which in no way compared to the screams of laughter from her loving mother, brother and sisters. Later Betty would laugh about this as well. Everyone in the Cahill household learned early and often the importance, and the joy, of laughing at themselves, engendering a healthy sense of humility.

Though ever ready for (and often the instigator of) a bit of light-hearted mischief, Mae remained, at her core, a strict disciplinarian and was consistently firm with her children. She never resorted to spanking but rather cultivated precious privileges in them and then punished bad behavior by denying those privileges one by one.

"My mother was not the best educated person in the world. But she was the most knowledgeable person in the world about every day life. How to get along, what you should and shouldn't do", recalled George. She impressed on them the practical aspects of how best to make one's way, stressing manners, honesty, integrity and hard work, and especially education. Mae had graduated high school herself, which was rare at the time she was growing up. But, oh, when it came to language, "I was not allowed to curse. Never. Cursing meant you didn't have a grasp of the English language. So there was no excuse for that."

Her practical example of hard work at both her jobs and at home — all while fostering a sense of humor in a difficult world — these were the hallmarks of Mae Cahill's life philosophy. And her children absorbed them well.

While Mae was working, Mary, Carolyn and Betty had each other to comfort and confide in as only sisters can. But being the only boy, George was left to his own devices. He had acquaintances in the neighborhood and at school, but not many steadfast friends. At home George talked easily with his sisters and they thoroughly enjoyed each other's company but they rarely traded confidences. By all accounts

George's relationship with every one of the girls was most affectionate and agreeable, with only the most occasional brotherly altercation.

Betty, the youngest, was shy and quietly reserved, not at all the outgoing social creature that Mary and Carolyn were. She kept to herself and was never far from home. She was not at all given to outbursts, at least not without being seriously provoked. One such provocation occurred on a lazy afternoon when Mae had gone out. George had done something only a brother could do to make a little sister very angry. So angry in fact, Betty picked up a heavy frying pan and swung it at him with a fury. When it connected with his head, he dropped to the floor and immediately played dead. Convinced she'd killed him, Betty became inconsolable and began wailing. After a couple minutes of this, when George popped up and revealed the ruse, she grabbed the pan and, to his delight, very much tried to hit him again.

For George this incident was a precious memory of Betty because she had, in all other respects, been a sedate and peaceable soul. He remembered her mostly holding to her mother rather than venturing out with the rest of the kids. And she absolutely could not bear to go to Florida with the others for their summer visits. Not that she didn't love her father, but rather her preference was for the comfort of home in the beloved company of Mae.

Mary, on the other hand, was something of a social butterfly who cultivated attachments with a fair number of boyfriends, some of whom she liked, and others she could take or leave. She wasn't one to be used by boys but rather was master and commander of her social life and woe be to he who tried to take advantage. On one occasion there was a boy with a car who'd asked Mary out to Belle Isle. Belle Isle was a popular family and dating site, a 900 acre island park in the middle of the Detroit River where one could rent canoes or little paddle boats to pedal around. The island also featured a lush conservatory, a well stocked aquarium, horse stables and a very nice stretch of beach.

Mary wanted to go but didn't care that much for the boy so she lied to him, declaring that, while her mother was working, she was responsible for her little brother and, if this boy wanted to go out with her, they would have to bring young George along. Begrudgingly the boy obliged and Mary and George — who was happy to join in on the scam — got to enjoy a day in the park. The boy had a portable Victrola and George's job was to keep it cranked up and playing records while they pedaled their paddle boat around. George of course helped himself to the picnic lunch the boy had packed. Mary and George continued to devise and execute many such delightful outings together, none of which benefitted her hopeful suitors, but all of which firmly cemented their own sibling relationship.

George remembered his sister Carolyn being a wonderful girl, although she didn't share with him quite the close-knit relationship that Mary enjoyed. At some point Carolyn acquired the nickname "Tillie". Where the label originated is unclear, though George suspected it may have been in reference to a popular comic strip of the time called "Tillie the Toiler[1]", which had also been turned into a 1927 silent movie of the same name starring Marion Davies as a stylish secretary and part-time model. Whatever the source, the name stuck and Carolyn wore it with pride from childhood on. Tillie was a tad more independent, serious, and even sophisticated for someone so young. She was also prodigiously athletic, always on the move, and a talented acrobatic dancer. George remembers looking up to her with great admiration. Just like her younger sister Mary, Tillie was quite popular and socialized with great aplomb.

---

1.   https://en.wikipedia.org/wiki/Tillie_the_Toiler

3

Chrysler

Mae had settled into a steady regimen continuing to work two jobs. Then one night at the dime-a-dance club she happened to be paired up with a customer named Jack Grant. Jack was a foreman at the Chrysler plant and had never been unemployed. He worked all through the depression supervising the manufacture of automobiles for the company's Dodge division. After a few weeks of acquaintanceship, the two of them formed an attachment. The taxi-dance club had a firm rule that dancers were not to date customers, but Mae and Jack saw each other on the sly anyway. After a courtship of just under a year, Jack and Mae married in 1934. Mae was not only able to quit the dance club, but left hat making behind forever as well. Jack had rented the second floor of a duplex for all of them to move into.

Young George and the girls easily warmed up to the arrangement and everyone got along quite nicely. Though the effects of the depression were still being felt, the marriage had significantly lessened the family's financial concerns and everyone was happy to bid farewell to Pauline. Of course after almost two years of imposing on the Hettricks' good graces, it was a genuine relief for Mae to be free of any obligation to her brother and finally have a place of her own. Jack was a very nice man, a good man, and there was certainly no competition for any of the affection George Jr. and the girls reserved for their father. They all got along well and Jack's attentions were wrapped up solely in keeping Mae and and the kids happy.

One day young George was playing stickball with some neighborhood kids in the alley behind the duplex and a fellow who lived a couple doors down came out and asked if he could join their game. His name was Don Nutting, an older boy by a few years. Don had his own car and operated an egg route. He used his car to deliver fresh eggs to houses in the area. He and George became friends.

Some weeks later, during one of their regular games behind the duplex, Mary came out to sit on the steps and watch them play. Being quite attractive, Mary often drew the attention of young men. Don asked pointedly, "Who is that girl?"

"That's my sister, Mary."

"Would you introduce me?"

So George obliged. And where none of her previous beaus had succeeded in winning her affections, Don seemed to hit it off with Mary right away.

Of course back in Florida, George Sr. was discovering a new romance of his own. In 1936 the children were pleased to discover George Sr. had married Flora Conoly in Jacksonville. The kids adored "Flo" and, during their summer visits, she warmed up to them as well. In fact, on September 18th 1939, Flo presented George Sr. with yet another daughter, Sandra Elizabeth Cahill ("Sandy"). According to a city directory of the time, they made a home together at 548 West 27th St, Apt. 2.

Having only been around since the early 1920's, the popularity of radio was not that old but its appeal had spread quickly. It was the cheapest form of public entertainment and only a few places, like stores, could afford to keep the radio on all the time since radio sets drew a great deal of electricity and their internal tubes had limited lifespans. A lot of stations didn't even broadcast beyond late hours of the evening. But by 1934, 60 percent of the nation's households had radios and one and a half million cars were outfitted with them. Up to that time world and local events reported by most newspapers consisted of news that was a day old. Now of course, when major happenings occurred, word of mouth sent up the alarm to "turn on the radio and listen for the news." Primarily though, radio was a source of entertainment.

Throughout its "Golden Age" of the 1930's, radio was so well liked that theaters dared not open until after the extremely popular *Amos 'n' Andy* radio program was over. These were the days of big budget broadcast productions exposing the public to a quality of entertainment they'd not previously known. Situation comedies and serialized radio plays employed top voice talents, image-inspiring sound effects and sophisticated music. In much the same fashion as reading held one's attention, radio engaged the consumer's imagination with dynamic visualization. And since most all the daytime serializations were sponsored by detergent companies, these radio plays quickly came to be known as "soap operas".

As a family, Mae, Jack and the kids enthusiastically tuned in to favorite weekly shows, with everyone gathered around the radio most evenings about 7:00. They delighted to the wholesome, broad-appeal broadcasts of *Jack Benny, Burns and Allen, Abbott and Costello, The 64 Thousand Dollar Question, Ellery Queen, Sam Spade, The Lone Ranger, Sherlock Holmes, The Shadow* and, of course, *Amos 'n' Andy*. Music programs were a particular favorite. The girls especially loved the week's Top Ten new songs, somehow already knowing all the words and singing along.

Come the weekend, the family often went to a Saturday Night double feature at a theater just a few blocks away. These were the days when movie theaters charged a small admission fee and patrons were welcome to stay as long as they pleased, rewatching a show over and over at no extra charge. Mae would pack a big lunch basket with food and bottled water and they'd all attend the evening's final double feature with cartoons, previews, newsreels and all. The logic in going to the last show on Saturday was that, at midnight, the theater changed the bill over to the coming week's double feature attraction. So the family stayed on, eating, drinking and enjoying four movies in a row with all the extras, from 9:30 Saturday night until around 2:00 Sunday morning — and thus the practice of "binging" was born. They didn't attend movies every week, but it was a frequent affair and, during the depression in Detroit, it was inexpensive and enjoyable family entertainment.

Books, music, movies and conversation were the popular cultural diversions of the day. Television would not present itself to the American public until the 1950's.

Unlike her two younger sisters, Carolyn could not tolerate Detroit. She longed for the bright, balmy climate of her beloved Florida and, as her father before her, put up with the north as long as she was able. At the end of her Junior year she begged to spend her last year of high school with her father in Jacksonville. Mae certainly didn't want to lose her, but when George Sr. agreed to take her in, she was obliged to let her daughter go, the first of her children to leave home. Carolyn returned to her beloved Florida where she would make her home for the rest of her life.

Some time around 1937 Jack was able to afford a house at 21457 Santa Clara Avenue in Redford, a safe, clean suburb of Detroit where the children would attend Redford High School. Mary and George always walked to school together and one morning, as they arrived at school, Mary said to George, "I'm going to talk to one of my girlfriends. You go on in."

George went inside but, through a big picture window, he could still see Mary outside. There was no girlfriend with her. And moments later Don Nutting's car pulled up, Mary scrambled in, and away they went to run his egg route together.

That afternoon when George arrived home from school, there was Mary, the picture of innocence.

"I saw you leave with Don this morning."

Mary was stricken. "Don't tell momma!"

Dutiful brother that he was, George kept her secret. But at a price. For some weeks after, at the dinner table, George continually asked, "Mary, can I have your dessert?" And of course Mary cheerfully handed it over to him amid curious looks from the family.

"She was very nice to me for a long time after that", George recalled with a chuckle.

While attending Redford High School, George Jr. wasn't overly academic but fared well enough with what he described as average grades. Extracurricular activities were few, although he's listed in his high school yearbook as Vice President of the Model Airplane Club. For a short time he and several boys built model aircraft and flew them in the park, perhaps envisioning himself one day a pilot. There was one boy at school named James Jackson with whom he formed a firm friendship. James was a good artist and in 1937 spontaneously drew a very nice portrait of him that he presented to George, a very quick sketch and a memorable tribute from a friend which he held onto for the rest of his life.

After school, George still managed a variety of jobs, mostly in grocery stores. There was another boy at school whose father ran a construction business and would often hire the two boys to tidy up newly finished houses by clearing trash, peeling stickers off freshly installed windows, cleaning and generally making the properties presentable for potential buyers. The two of them also took jobs cutting grass.

Not far from where the they lived in Redford were public stables that rented horses and, with the first couple of rental sessions, the owners provided a young man to ride along with them, instructing the teenagers on rudimentary horsemanship. They picked it up quickly and, for the next year and a half or so, the three Cahill children went on an equestrian craze. George, Betty, Mary (and Don too) bought all the outfits and spent hundreds of hours on the many beautiful horse trails that wound through the city's outskirts.

One of the perks of working for Chrysler was that sons of employees (but not daughters) were welcome to apply for a summer program offered by the company called the **Chrysler Boys Tour**. With Jack being a long time Chrysler man, George was eligible, applying to the program in 1937 and 1938. Participation was limited to 200 boys, so it was something special when he was finally accepted in 1939.

For the tour, Chrysler provided each of the boys two identical uniforms; one uniform to wear while the other was being cleaned. Also provided were adult supervisors driving ten large canvas-covered Dodge transport trucks where the boys, in military fashion, rode in the back, about 20 to a truck.

For two wonderful weeks that summer these lucky teenagers visited sites of national interest throughout the northeastern U.S. and were introduced to parts of America beyond their experience. Every evening the trucks would arrive at a previously designated camp ground at which an advance team had set up massive tents where the boys would eat and sleep. Soiled uniforms were handed over for cleaning by a unit that traveled with them and facilities for bathing were made available as well. All amenities were met and numerous sights were seen. It was a grand adventure for many young men who would otherwise never get out of the city.

The easternmost stop on the Chrysler Boys Tour this year would be the 1939 World's Fair[1] at Flushing Meadows in Queens, New York where the boys would spend a couple of days enjoying the fair's many modern exhibits. One exhibit in particular featured the exotic fan dancing of a Sally Rand-type troupe of ladies called the Crystal Lassies[2].

---

1. https://www.youtube.com/watch?v=HcfgvzwaDHc

2. https://www.youtube.com/watch?v=qHbG-2M1zfI

Being all of 16 years old, George would not be granted admission to this very adult attraction — darn it!

Having lived mostly with her Aunt Bessie during her Senior year in Jacksonville, Carolyn graduated from Jackson High School where she had continued her acrobatic dancing, performed in several school musicals, and made quite a name for herself on the girls basketball team, even being mentioned as a star player in the Florida Times-Union newspaper. After school she went to work for the Gulf Life Insurance Company and, in 1936 met Harry Clark Hardwick ("Butch") when she flatly ignored a sign at Jacksonville Beach warning: DO NOT TALK TO THE LIFEGUARDS. Butch was of course going to get talked to by Carolyn and no one was going to stop her. After a whirlwind courtship, Carolyn and Butch exchanged vows at a Judge's residence beside the Old St. Augustine Lighthouse. Butch didn't tell his parents about the marriage for a year because he so feared their reaction.

In the summer of 1939, the two of them took a road trip from Florida to Michigan to see Mary, Betty, Mae and Jack. The visit was strategic in that it would coincide with the time George was to be traveling with the Chrysler Boys Tour. After a bit of time letting Mae and Jack get acquainted with their new son-in-law, Carolyn and Butch would have Mary join them as they continued on to New York. There Butch and the girls would meet up with their little brother and all enjoy the World's Fair together. George had arranged in advance, with written permission from his mother, to part from the boys tour after New York and join his sisters on their return road trip back to Detroit.

Upon the threesome's arrival in New York they were stunned to see Don Nutting who had driven there on his own to surprise Mary. Don joined them to take in the World's Fair and, promptly afterward, drove back to Detroit on his own. There is a snapshot taken by Tillie during this 1939 meet up in New York showing Don with the group outside a restaurant. It's also one of the few rare photographs of 16-year-old George Jr. in his Chrysler Boys Tour uniform.

Butch and Carolyn's car had a rumble seat which would be exposed to the weather so Butch rigged a shaded covering for Mary and George who spent the trip back to Detroit enjoying the fresh air and scenery from the rumble seat. It was an adventurous, carefree summer for them all.

George Jr.'s modest dreams had long led him to believe that life as an engineer would be ideal. Inspired by intrepid characters from the books of his youth, he imagined traveling the world designing and building things — what could be better? But it had only ever been a fantasy since engineering required a college degree. And who could afford college? Jack Grant offered a more pedestrian alternative, recommending tool-and-die making as a creative and rewarding occupation. He declared that every tool-and-die man at Chrysler made very good money and had a great job for life.

In early 1941, not long out of Redford High School, George followed Jack's advice and applied to Chrysler's two year tool-and-die training program. It paid 50-cents an hour and very quickly turned into the most monotonously repetitive, soul-sucking waste of time. Yes, a tool-and-die maker needed to learn assembly line processes as part of his education, but the monumental tedium of this so-called training was beyond mind numbing. All day, every day, George stood in a single spot. He'd take a small part designed for automobile brakes from a bin on his left, mill a minor portion of it to specification on the lathe in front of him, toss the part into a bin on the right, and then take an identical small part from the bin on the left again, mill it the same way on the lathe again, toss it into the bin on the right again, and so on. And so on. Hour after hour. Day after day... after day...

Don Nutting was faring a bit better, having landed a good job manufacturing boxes with the Ex-Cell-O Corporation in Detroit. In fact he was doing well enough that, on the Saturday before Thanksgiving 1940, he and Mary formally traded wedding vows, and George now had a second brother-in-law.

The war in Europe had been going on for over a year, ever since Germany's invasion of Poland in September of '39. Through the Lend Lease Act[3], the United States had been busy supplying its European allies with military vehicles and other hardware to defend themselves. As a highly crucial manufacturing center for this activity, Detroit was one of the handful of key U.S. industrial hubs referred to collectively by President Roosevelt as the "Arsenal of Democracy[4]". In addition to its considerable commercial and military manufacturing commitments, Chrysler landed a massive contract with the War Department to build armored tanks.

In February of 1941 ground was broken on the construction of an enormous new factory, the Chrysler Tank Arsenal[5], on a 200 acre piece of ground in the farming township of Warren, Michigan, just 17 miles outside Detroit. By July 1941 the arsenal was up and running, hiring 200 workers a day to staff the facility. The gigantic new structure had been paid for and was owned by the government, but it had been designed and constructed to Chrysler's specifications and the machinery inside would be purchased and operated by the company as well. It's work force would rapidly grow to 5000.

Chrysler's company policy was to post job opportunities internally before offering them to the public. After six months of tedium, George was no longer able to stomach the tool-and-die "training" program.

---

3. https://en.wikipedia.org/wiki/Lend-Lease

4. https://en.wikipedia.org/wiki/Arsenal_of_Democracy

5.   https://vimeo.com/358619967

When he saw a posting on the job board for the new tank arsenal, it was his ticket out. He applied and was brought on to work at the new facility in Warren.

Without a car of his own, George had been relying on Jack Grant as his ride to and from the tool-and-die training gig. But the new job in Warren was quite a distance further and, at the time, Jack had been talking about buying a new car. Rather than trading in his old Dodge, George offered to buy it from him on a payment plan. Jack agreed and, for a price of $50.00, George had his first car.

At Chrysler's massive tank arsenal, where the last of the M3 tanks and the brand new M4 General Sherman tanks were being assembled, George and one other man became lords of the Tool Crib, a job thankfully unburdened by monotony. The two young men doled out specially requested items to the workers and conscientiously tracked every single tool, each of which was catalogued on a series of immense boards throughout the massive caged area. To check out a tool from the crib, such as a micrometer or torque wrench, each worker surrendered a hole-punched metal disk with their employee number stamped into it. The disk was hung in place of the borrowed tool and, at the end of a shift, if a tool had not been returned, the two crib masters would track down the offending party, retrieve the tool and return the employee's disk. Every tool, without exception had to be returned or the employee would be charged its replacement cost, which was considerable. In all his time there, never once did George permit a tool to go missing.

At the time of his birth in 1922, George's parents hadn't quite yet settled on a name for him, so the Name line on his birth certificate simply read "Baby" Cahill. As this was the document provided for proof of age when applying for the tool crib job, word got out. As a result, throughout his tenure at Chrysler, George would be known as "baby in the crib". (His official certificate of birth was later amended with his correct legal name.)

First thing every morning at the tank arsenal there was a rush of workers anxious to check out the day's hardware. With only two men in the tool crib, the day began as a high speed madhouse but George and his fellow crib mate handled the demand with capable efficiency. Returning tools at the end of the shift became the same mad rush but in reverse. Middle hours were easier as only occasional tool requests came and went.

George found the job most interesting and learned a lot about tools. During the day he found time to stroll through the plant watching the hardware in action and was able to observe at close quarters exactly how these massive war machines were assembled. He regularly toured the testing grounds outside where the tanks were run through their paces to certify them as battle ready, watching them navigate steep grades, crash through rough brush, and roar through deep troughs and streams.

A condition of employment required him to join the union, so the pay of course was an enormous improvement over his previous salary. As a company man, and being entitled to a company discount, George soon traded in the second hand Dodge he'd acquired from Jack Grant and bought himself a brand New Plymouth sedan from a local dealership on the easy payment plan. The car cost him $800.00. Having struggled through the Great Depression, things were finally taking quite a turn for the better.

Life was good.

Early one bright Sunday afternoon, just as George, Betty, Mary and Don were returning from the movies, they arrived home to discover Mae and Jack riveted to the radio, listening to breaking news of an attack. Throughout the rest of the day they followed closely the numerous devastating reports of death and destruction resulting from a Japanese bombing raid on Pearl Harbor[6] in Hawaii. It was December

7th 1941. Though the unprovoked assault on an American base on American soil was all anyone could think about, it is worth noting that, on the same day, the Japanese were simultaneously attacking Midway, Guam and the Philippines, plus a number of other vulnerable targets in the Pacific. The United States had been gearing up for war but wasn't presently prepared to engage so bold an enemy in such a vicious and unprovoked assault.

The following day President Roosevelt addressed congress and made his historic "A Date That Will Live in Infamy[7]" speech. Though everyone had understood for some time that America would eventually be drawn into the Second World War, it was no less a shock when this cataclysmic event forced the country's hand. On December 11th 1941, just three days after Roosevelt's speech, Adolf Hitler and Benito Mussolini announced that Germany and Italy were declaring war on the United States. And just that quickly the life of every single American had been staggeringly altered forever.

Chrysler immediately stopped building cars. All its facilities became solely dedicated to supplying the American war effort. Now that America was in the fight, its previously steady stream of imported parts and supplies was reduced to practically nothing and all domestic iron and steel stocks were suddenly marshaled for U.S. defense. As the Yankees were suddenly part of the war, American exports, so desperately relied upon by European Allied forces, were now radically reduced. Planes, ships, military vehicles and munitions for its own defense were primarily what America would be manufacturing for the foreseeable future. Every single non-military business or concern requiring metal, glass, mechanical services and fuel were going to have to wait. No new cars, no stoves, refrigerators, washers, water heaters, furnaces or machines of any kind were being made for public

---

6. https://vimeo.com/487806275

7.   https://www.c-span.org/video/?419693-1/president-roosevelts-day-infamy-address-congress

consumption. All was in service to the manufacture and maintenance of military goods, and the few commodities of a non-military nature that did remain were quickly bought up. You couldn't get a plumber or electrician because wire, metal pipe, fittings and fixtures were suddenly unavailable. Everything in the nation was redirected to the war effort — both materials and manpower. Community drives to collect scrap metal, glass and paper were conducted across the nation and recycling went into overdrive to bolster dwindling supplies. For many, having only just emerged from a Great Depression, such deprivations were hardly bearable. Now these scarcities would be pressing on for the foreseeable future. Possibly years.

Less than two weeks after the United States entered World War II, amendments to the Selective Training and Service Act [8]suddenly made all men between the ages of 20 and 44 liable for military service, should the need arise. It was also mandated that every male between the ages of 18 and 64 register their eligibility to be drafted into military service. George Jr. dutifully complied, as did his Father, even though George Sr. had previously served in World War I.

The "Great War" or "The War to End All Wars", as the conflict of 1914 to 1918 had come to be known, had also begun on foreign shores and America had only been drawn into it during its final stages. But Germany and Austria-Hungary had begun fighting the allied countries of England, France and Russia in the summer of 1914. From the first, President Woodrow Wilson made it clear the U.S. would remain neutral despite repeated congressional debates and tests of our country's tolerance — especially when Germany sank the British passenger liner Lusitania on May 7th, 1915 killing more than 120 U.S. citizens. Some two years later, only after Germany repeated and then escalated its attacks on American ships, was the United States finally

---

8.   https://en.wikipedia.org/wiki/Selective_Training_and_Service_Act_of_1940

compelled to stand up with Allied forces and, on April 6, 1917, declare war on Germany.

The U.S. would send more than a million troops off to Europe, where they arrived in the middle of a war unlike any the world had ever seen — one waged in trenches and in the air, and marked by the rise of such military technologies as the tank, the modern grenade and poison gas.

1917 had been a pivotal year for George Sr. As a recent newlywed, he and Mae Iverine Hettrick lost their newborn baby girl Margaret (named after Mae's mother) when she was just three weeks old. Then, shortly after his 18th birthday, George Sr. joined the United States Navy to fight in World War I. Having completed basic training as a pharmacist's mate, he was scheduled to be shipped off to Europe. However, as he climbed the narrow gangplank to board his ship, he lost his footing, resulting in a great fall and a badly broken leg. During recovery in the hospital the injury developed into gangrene and doctors declared the leg must come off.

"Absolutely not!"

George Sr. was adamant. There was no way he would ever allow an amputation.

"Suit yourself," they said.

And he did.

The wound somehow healed and in time George Sr. recovered the full use of the leg. So much so that it would never be the slightest impediment to his lifelong devotion to athletics. Compounding his bad luck during this interval, he soon contracted a bout of yellow jaundice and was sent home by the Navy to recover. Not long after, on November 11th 1918, an armistice agreement was signed. The war was over and the entire world knew its children would never again be forced to endure such a devastating conflict.

And yet, a scant 23 years later, World War II was well underway. Though George Sr. was never called to duty for this conflict, he remained active in the U.S. Coast Guard Temporary Reserve and, throughout the war, did volunteer patrol work around Jacksonville Harbor.

George Sr.'s son was doing his part as a civilian in Michigan, contributing to the manufacture of tanks for the war effort. All of America followed closely, even hourly, the escalating conflicts abroad as well as the mounting casualties. Every day newspaper and radio reports related the grim specifics of bloody battles, bombing victims, hand-to-hand combat and soldiers being bayoneted in trenches. First hand news accounts awakened Americans much too abruptly to the unvarnished horrors of a global conflict that was suddenly all too personal.

The machinery of war was consuming people at an alarming rate and all around him in Detroit young men were disappearing daily to the draft. Young George knew his number would shortly be up and he did not want to wind up as regular infantry in a trench somewhere. If he was going to be part of this conflict, he at least wanted to have some say in how he was to be involved.

4

Putting to Sea

After agonizing over it for some weeks, George Jr. finally made the difficult decision to quit his job at the Chrysler tank arsenal, drive to Florida, take a brief vacation to visit with his father, and then enlist, preferably in a more specialized branch of the service.

A few weeks shy of his 20th birthday — the date he would become eligible for the draft — George bid a sad farewell to his family, plotted his course on a map, and set out for Florida. On the last leg of his trip, passing from Georgia into Florida, his Plymouth was getting low on gas and, when he stopped to fill up, the attendant at the gas station asked for his ration coupons.

"Ration coupons...?"

With the war on, many regions imposed rationing to conserve fuel supplies. No coupons, no gas. The attendant suggested George drive back north about 50 miles, just beyond the point where rationing began, top off his tank there and buy some gas cans to fill up so he could make it to Jacksonville. He followed the advice and eventually arrived at his father and Flo's where he could take his ease for a while and weigh enlistment strategies.

Young George's first consideration was the Marines. He and Don Nutting's nephew, who was staying with them at the time, both decided to apply together. Every enlistment office had its own doctors who conducted physicals on the spot. George was immediately rejected owing to his unnaturally high insteps. He was told his feet would not bear up under the weight of a backpack loaded with heavy equipment and he'd likely break down in the field. Don's nephew, on the other hand, was accepted as a marine and later ended up being badly wounded during fighting in the Pacific. He survived the war but would be ailed the rest of his life by serious injuries that never quite healed.

George then thought he'd perhaps make a good pilot and applied to the Naval Air Corps. After his physical exam he was rejected there as well — a slight overbite meant he wouldn't be able to wear a pilot's specifically fitted oxygen mask. He later learned that a large number of pilots got killed in training while learning to land on aircraft carriers and thereafter considered his overbite something of a small blessing.

During this period George's father had been associating with a great number of enlisted men and was friends with two chief bosuns mates who were seeking new recruits for the Navy. George Sr. prompted the men for details, discovering that a typical recruit starts out at the lowest rank of Apprentice Seaman. However, if one had experience, say, with boats and sailing, they were likely to be quickly promoted to a higher pay and rank. As, perhaps, Seaman 1st Class.

"Well, my son knows boats and sailing", declared George. Of course, it wasn't the case at all. The boy knew nothing of boats and sailing, at least not beyond operating one of the paddle boats at Belle Isle.

After sharing the recruiters' insights, George Jr. agreed to apply. The two chief bosuns mates were on the lookout for their friend's son and, sure enough, in early October of '42, once he'd passed his physical and was accepted, the men made good on their word and George Cahill Jr. was offered entry into the U.S. Navy with the promise of quick promotion.

Ironically, mere days later, on October 11, 1942 George received a draft notice from the U.S. War Department instructing him to report for duty with the U.S. Army. Having only just been approved for enlistment in the Navy, but not yet being 21, George would need a signed notarized letter of permission from his legal guardian — his mother. On October 12th he fired off a letter to her, along with a Navy form to approve his induction, and requested a speedy response.

Mae did not want her only son going off to war but ultimately accepted the awful truth that, if he didn't join up now, he would be bound to the army where his circumstances would be less certain. She gave her consent and air mailed the form he had sent.

Just over a week later, on Wednesday October 21st 1942 George Newton Cahill Jr. reported for duty at Mayport Naval Station about 15 miles northeast of Jacksonville. Upon his arrival he presented his birth certificate as proof of age.

When Mae Cahill had gone into labor on September 4th 1922, the process of giving birth took its sweet time, as labor often can, until just after midnight when George Jr. was born. But in his parents' minds, the birth had taken place on the 4th, the date on which his birthday would be celebrated all growing up. It wasn't until he presented his birth certificate for proof of age at basic training that it was finally pointed out his actual date of birth was the 5th of September.

"So now I celebrate on both the 4th and the 5th," George would later remark with a grin.

Basic training routinely ran about eight-to-ten weeks but, owing to the timing of his enlistment, George's class had begun a week before his arrival so there was some catching up to do, including an inordinate number of requisite inoculations. Instead of spacing these boosters out over several days, as was common practice, the decision was made to catch him up with the class. George received all his shots in one day, using large-bore 1940's hypodermics, not at all like the hair-thin needles common today. The injections were excruciating and, for almost the entirety of the next week, he was completely unable to lift either arm.

During his induction physical at Mayport, a particularly craven doctor made note of all recruits who had not previously benefitted from a common practice and unceremoniously declared, "All you fellas who haven't been circumcised — you're gonna get circumcised."

With no discussion whatsoever, the deed was done.

As a grown man undergoing such an inordinately painful procedure, the several days of recovery in sickbay meant even the slightest movement triggered the most electrifying pain. Of course, a well meaning friend, knowing George's love of reading, brought him a copy of "*A Tree Grows in Brooklyn*" by Betty Smith. As George later recalled, "It was the funniest book I'd ever read — and it almost KILLED me." Ironically, and owing to the excellent writing and storytelling, it became and remained his favorite book ever.

George's instructor for basic training was an older, retired bosun's mate who'd been called back to the Navy specifically to train recruits. The poor fellow had a bad ulcer and was always drinking canned milk to ease the discomfort. George remembered him fondly as a really good guy who absolutely "knew his stuff." The man did an excellent job of guiding the boys through their paces, teaching them to run drills and master the crucial basics of seamanship. It was all brand new to George, developing a set of skills he never knew existed.

For water survival they were instructed how to remove their sailor's wide-legged bell bottom pants, tie the bottoms of the legs together, then slap the tops down onto the water's surface to fill them with air for use as a floatation device[1]. The captured air lasted several minutes before leaking out through the thick wet fabric, but it was enough to give a survivor a good rest before having to slap them down and refill the air again. For innumerable sailors over the years surviving the sinking of a ship, this tactic has saved many from a watery demise.

George recalled the food at Mayport as being very good. Best pies and cakes he'd ever had. Chow at sea however was a different story altogether. In his experience, shipboard fare was remarkably unpalatable.

---

1.   https://www.youtube.com/watch?v=oNTSoKg6xHM

The patrol boats to which he was assigned were old World War I sub chasers. These 110-foot-long wooden vessels were very slender craft originally built for speed, despite the fact that German subs were much faster underwater than these boats were on the surface. The boats were not possessed of much girth and rocked incessantly in rough waters. On his first ocean tour the water was quite choppy and George immediately got seasick, an horrendous bout that simply wouldn't let up. After a day or so, the crew finally tied him to the railing on deck to let him keep throwing up over the side until he just couldn't throw up any more, all while the boat relentlessly flopping back and forth in the choppy surf. He remembered praying desperately that a huge wave would come and sink the ship so he could just die and be done with it. That first patrol lasted about a week. Somehow, over the course of future tours at sea, George eventually adapted.

Cutting off an enemy's supplies during wartime is an age old tactic and remains a common military practice. Since the bulk of international trade to America was conducted by sea, German submarines were torpedoing every American ship they could find. Just a few miles off shore, U.S. shipping lanes were littered with hundreds of wrecks all up and down the eastern seaboard, many of them in shallow enough water to be an obstruction to unsuspecting surface vessels. An especially hazardous stretch was along the North Carolina coast which earned the grim nickname Torpedo Alley[2]. Over 400 Allied commercial, military and merchant marine ships were sunk and 5000 lives lost along the U.S. Atlantic coast during World War II.

While larger and more robust cruisers and destroyers were better equipped to engage a submerged enemy, the Navy relied heavily on as many craft as could be mustered, large or small, military or privately

---

2. https://en.wikipedia.org/wiki/Torpedo_Alley

owned, to be their eyes on the water along every coast, sounding the alarm at the slightest sign of enemy presence.

For much of his first year of seafaring service, George Jr. served on two vintage World War I wooden sub chasers; the **USS YP459** and the **USS YP17**. The "Y" descriptor stood for a "Yacht" class vessel. While several actual private yachts had indeed been pressed into service as submarine lookouts, and though neither of George's two sub chasers was technically a yacht, such was the military designation, referring to the crafts' relative size and shape. The "P" descriptor represented the vessel's employment for "Patrol" purposes, though they were more commonly referred to as "Pogey Boats".

Neither of the two boats to which Seaman 1st Class Cahill was assigned merited an actual captain so a lieutenant was assigned to their command. There were relatively few armaments kept aboard the old sub chasers and the boys had been run through only the briefest class in weapons. Each Pogey boat stocked some old Springfield .30-06 rifles that were only occasionally brought out by the men to kill sharks. There were also a few .45 automatic side arms, which almost never came out, plus a small stash of old depth charges left over from the First World War, but no one paid them any mind. Finally the deck had been outfitted with a 20mm gun; nothing that would repel an enemy ship or submarine but a substantial enough weapon to offer some small measure of defense in an emergency.

The Navy didn't want these sub chasers confronting the enemy. Rather, their mission was strictly observational, sent out to spot subs and then radio in a location so the Naval Air Corps could bomb them. Employed in this regard, the expansive fleet of American sub chasers was the Navy's most prolific front line effort in U.S. coastal warnings against enemy subs. It was a crucial and dangerous duty. George's boats covered territory cruising south from Jacksonville down to the tip of Florida, then all the way north to the Carolinas and finally back south again to Mayport, with patrols lasting anywhere from two-to-five days each. Neither of the two ships on which George served ever maintained a consistent crew. As a result, transferring crew members came and went all the time.

Electronic equipment on submarines at the time was battery powered. These batteries only held a charge for a day, maybe a day and a half, thus it was crucial for enemy subs to surface regularly so they could fire up their onboard diesel generators to recharge the batteries. Since it was more hazardous to be topside in daylight, German and Japanese submariners would mostly surface at night when visibility was reduced. George's crew was therefore more likely to happen upon a surfaced German or Japanese submarine in the dark. It's fortunate they never did.

The U.S. Office of Civil Defense was established in May 1941 and, throughout the war, cities along the U.S. coast were under strict blackout orders. Through stern warnings with posters, flyers and radio announcements, Americans were constantly reminded to cover and/ or minimize nighttime lighting. After the bombing of Pearl Harbor, people across the nation took more seriously the threat of domestic attacks. Blackout curtains were mandated to cover windows in homes and businesses on land, and the dousing of streetlights became even more crucial since oceangoing vessels became ready enemy targets when silhouetted against lights on shore. To avoid being spotted, all ships and watercraft were required to operate at night with no running lights whatsoever, a defensive measure that generated its own hazards.

Night patrols on the water were incredibly dangerous since a good number of large, fast moving vessels came and went in the dark and, without running lights, the likelihood of collisions with larger ships and the running over of smaller ships was not only high but unfortunately common. Surface craft at sea signaled each other at night by flashing light signals through long directional tubes on deck. One ship would flash a hailing message through one of these signal tubes and the receiving ship was required to flash a reply.

One moonless, pitch black night, George's sub chaser happened upon a large silhouette and flashed a standard hailing signal. There was no acknowledgement. They hailed a second and a third time, still with no response. Finally the lieutenant commanded, "Throw a spotlight on that ship and let's see who these guys are."

It was a massive U.S. Navy frigate. Immediately a voice boomed across the water from a loud speaker: "PUT THAT LIGHT OUT OR WE'RE GONNA BLOW YOU OUTTA THE WATER!"

The light went out and the smaller craft quietly turned and disappeared into the night.

Prior to America's involvement in the war, the German navy had steadily wrought havoc on all non-axis ships in the North Atlantic from 1940 to 1941, a period Hitler's generals referred to as "The First Happy Time" because their assaults were mostly unopposed. As a direct result of Hitler and Mussolini declaring war on the U.S. on December 11th of '41, the axis navies could begin their "Second Happy Time[3]", also laughingly known among German submarine commanders as "American Shooting Season". On December 12th Adolf Hitler ordered a direct and full out naval assault along the east coast of the United States officially titled Operation Drumbeat, lasting from January through August 1942 when American defenses were still weak and not yet fully organized.

America's enemies were pulling no punches and German and Japanese subs aggressively sank everything that floated all along the U.S. coast, from small water craft and banana boats to freight liners, passenger ships and military vessels. Torpedoes were in limited supply and reserved for the largest ships. But for medium sized and smaller boats, the subs would surface and tear them to pieces with cannon fire and machine guns, a merciless and all-too-common occurrence.

---

3. https://en.wikipedia.org/wiki/Second_Happy_Time

When any U.S. ship was sunk, it was the immediate duty of a Pogey boat to travel to the site and transmit confirmation of the downed vessel's precise location to the Hydrographic office. For most lost ships, other than surface debris at the site, there'd be little visible evidence of the craft itself and a scan was often relied upon to render a detailed subsurface grid location, using an early form of sonar with which all American naval ships were now equipped.

On occasion, owing to the relative shallowness of the water, a ship's wreckage might not have gone fully underwater. And for vessels that were completely submerged, when the water was clear enough, portions of a lifeless craft, if not its entirety, could be seen just below the surface. Sections of masts, guns or conning towers might jut up to within five to ten feet of the surface as potentially dangerous obstructions to larger fast moving surface vessels. It was crucial that these hazards be carefully recorded and accurately charted by the Hydrographic Office. Regularly updated charts were constantly being distributed to all Navy craft operating in shipping lanes to safely avoid fresh obstructions in waters already densely littered with wrecks.

For Pogey boats sent to investigate these wrecks, knowing they'd only just been torpedoed and with all victims still aboard, surveying a site was always a deeply disturbing experience. Just hours earlier, this had been a vital seagoing vessel with a full and lively crew.

"A lot of them are still down there today", George recalled.

In such moments he never felt more far removed from any sense of home — nor ever closer to family.

Late in 1943, his Pogey boat's lieutenant became convinced they'd located a submerged enemy submarine. Though regulations were explicit that they were to take no action and should only radio in the location for bomber planes, the lieutenant declared, "We're gonna get this guy. Prepare two depth charges."

The crew eyed each other for a long moment. Then begrudgingly followed his orders and lined the boat up over the suspected target's position. During this operation George was in the cabin near the lieutenant and the pilot. On board were four rusty, 25-year-old depth charges left over from the 1st World War and no one present had ever done this before, or even seen it done. In fact their only depth charge training had consisted of a single, brief anecdotal explanation of how the process was supposed to work... in theory. Nothing more.

One depth charge was mounted on each of the two rail systems that ran along either side of the boat. Depth was estimated, depth settings were dialed into the two charges and, on the lieutenant's command, the rail blocks were removed. As these two large drums of TNT rolled off the back of the boat, the pilot gunned the motor — and the engine stopped.

Along with every heart on board.

George's sub chaser was dead in the water directly above what, in moments, would be a massive double explosion that would surely turn their craft to splinters. The pilot tried and tried, eventually restarting the engines, well after the explosion ought have occurred. But it never did. Instead these two ancient, faulty explosives had sunk quietly into the mud at the bottom of the Atlantic, where they likely remain today.

"Talk about a bunch of guys who absolutely knew they were about to die", George recalled.

The crew collectively exhaled and the lieutenant suddenly thought better of his decision, agreeing with others aboard that they had really only detected a whale and not a sub.

For one ten-day leave, Mae and Jack had purchased a plane ticket for George to come home to Detroit. He was proud to be his mother's son in uniform and happy to once again be close to those he loved. During this visit Mae had gone to the grocery store alone and, while a bag boy at the store was helping her to the car with her groceries, the young man made a nasty remark about Mae's appearance, implying she was shabby. It cut her to the quick as she had only ever presented and maintained herself with modest decorum and great care.

When George heard of this he insisted they return to the store the next day to confront the offending party. When they arrived, George asked for the manager, fully prepared to give the kid what for. The deeply apologetic manager confessed the boy no longer worked there. He'd been dismissed the day before for doing the exact same thing to another customer. Though gratified that the offender had been fired, George held only the smallest regret that he was denied the opportunity to personally vindicate his mother's honor.

After a year patrolling in open water on Pogey boats, George felt his talents would be better employed in the Hydrographic Office and applied for a promotion to Quartermaster. Four weeks later when the application was approved, he bid farewell to his shipmates and took up a month's training back at Mayport.

The naval station's Hydrographic office was a hive of activity with a staff of four constantly maintaining, revising and circulating the most up to date navigational charts for every shipping lane up and down the eastern seaboard. One of George's jobs was to receive, verify and record new information on the latest victims of enemy attack. Once a wreck's precise location was authenticated, its coordinates, along with any danger it might pose to ship travel, were updated on all pertinent charts. Reports of new wrecks came in frequently, almost daily.

While the quartermaster's office was primarily in service to the security of American navy craft, the division also permitted access to these records by a few civilian companies that regularly required copies. These companies would reproduce and distribute newly revised charts (for a fee) to merchant marine and commercial vessels operating in

U.S. coastal waters, since non-military water craft relied equally on the navy's updates for their own safe navigation. George would spend the next year and a half dedicated to ensuring the accuracy and timeliness of charts issued by this office, as so many American lives depended on them.

As an ancillary benefit to his new shore duty at Mayport, George enjoyed a more regular schedule that left him with many weekends free. He would hitchhike the half hour into Jacksonville and spend time with his father or visit with his cousin Frank.

Mary and Don's son Mickey had been born eight weeks before Pearl Harbor on October 4th 1941, so Mary was happy to have her little boy's father close to home for much of the war. At the beginning of the war, Don Nutting's company, Ex-Cell-O Corporation, had won a government contract and switched from making boxes to manufacturing tank parts. As his particular job suddenly qualified as military support, Don's position exempted him from the draft. Once the contract was completed however, he would be eligible to be shipped overseas. Though he never ended up seeing active duty, Don later lamented to George Jr. his sincere regret at not being part of the action abroad.

During the many drives south with Mae to deliver the kids for their summer visits with George Sr., Jack Grant had developed a preference for the sunny climes of Florida and eventually agreed with Mae that they had endured enough Michigan winters. Jack retired from Chrysler and he and Mae moved to the sunshine state to run their own motel. Don and Mary declared they too wanted to move to Florida and suggested they all transplant themselves together.

Mae and Jack, along with Betty who had just graduated Redford High School, took little Mickey Nutting with them in their car for the drive down. Mary and Don followed shortly after. They all spent a week in Orlando, Florida to see if the locale suited them. Ultimately they favored the gulf coast and decided to settle in the Tampa/St. Petersburg area where they purchased a motel in which Jack and Mae took up residence while they ran it. Jack also bought a house at 917 West Woodlawn Avenue in nearby St. Petersburg. It was a little two-bedroom single bath place with a nice sun room and a tiny kitchen. That's where Don, Mary and little Mickey were living when their second child Linda was born.

Like her sister Carolyn before her, Betty landed a job in Jacksonville with the Gulf Life Insurance Company. In her free time she'd go to dances and, being so close to Mayport, there were always plenty of navy boys in attendance. In early November 1945, during one such dance at the local USO (United Service Organization[4]), Betty Long introduced her cousin Betty Cahill to a sailor named Bob McFarland and the two started dating. Not too long after, Bob invited Betty to an open house on the ship he was assigned to. Small launches would ferry visitors out to the ships anchored on St. John's River. As instructed by Bob, when she arrived at the docks she was only to mention who she was there to see and they would know which ship to take her to. Everyone knew Bob and he was well liked. When Betty dropped his name the crew was only too glad to run her out to his ship on a motor launch.

Betty had decked herself out in one of her most attractive dresses to look her best for the occasion. As the launch pulled up to Bob's ship, she was met with a startling challenge. The only way to get aboard was to climb the 18-or-so feet up a densely woven cargo net that was draped over the ship's side, and then, at the top, climb over a railing.

Incredulous she declared, "I can't climb that."

"Sure you can!"

After taking a minute to figure out the logistics of the thing, this traditionally reserved young girl in her prettiest dress went for it. She

---

4.   https://en.wikipedia.org/wiki/United_Service_Organizations#World_War_II

grabbed handful after handful of thick rope and carefully stepped up, one high heel after another, rung after rung, all the way to the top of the net with an excited crew above cheering her on and a more excited crew on the launch below enjoying the view. With some assistance at the last, she finally climbed over the railing and was cheered. A deafening cheer.

As it turned out, of all the girlfriends, wives and relatives who'd been invited to the ship's open house, Betty was the one and only female intrepid enough to make an appearance. As the lone woman aboard that day, she was treated as true royalty. The officers even deemed to mix with the men and the captain himself showed Betty every courtesy at his command. Bob was now more popular than ever. When it came time to depart and Betty repeated her feat, this time in reverse, admiration for her only soared. Everyone absolutely loved Betty.

And Betty absolutely loved Bob.

So much so that, after knowing him barely six weeks, she eloped with him three days after Christmas 1945 and came back home to tell her dad.

"We got married!"

George Sr. was incredibly upset about it, declaring, "It'll never last. Never!" Unfazed by her father's disapproval, the happy couple went on a brief honeymoon, heading up to Detroit so her mother and Jack could meet Bob. The couple ended up staying there until August of 1946. Bob had completed his service with the Navy in May and, with summer winding down, it was time to travel to California to introduce Betty to Bob's family. In December Bob and Betty returned to Tampa, Florida, driving a Packard convertible. They had hoped to have the top down all the way but at that time Texas was experiencing the worst winter in its history.

Butch Hardwick, much like his wife Carolyn, had always been physically active. He was a great water guy. In fact he was a marathon swimmer in addition to being a lifeguard at the public beach. Like two of his brothers-in-law, George and Bob, he was a Navy man as well. Butch was destined to be a seafaring fellow all his life and after the war he would remain in the auxiliary Navy. Though all the Cahill women had settled their love lives irrevocably, romance had been slower to blossom for George Jr. — but only slightly.

Some year's before, George Sr.'s sister Bessie had married Fred Long. Together Bessie and Fred had three sons; Fred Jr., Frank and Jack, plus two girls, Betty and Helen, all of them the most delightful of people whom George Jr. visited a lot. The Longs had a beautiful house on Trout River in the very nice suburb of Lake Forest just outside Jacksonville. Fred Sr. was a salesman for the Groover-Stewart Drug company, the same firm where George's father had worked before the Depression. Being in sales and constantly traveling on company business, Fred's car had seen far better days and was in quite bad shape. During the war, and for some time after, it was still impossible to purchase a new vehicle. There were simply none available. After joining the navy George knew he wouldn't be using his own car so he had put it in storage. Hearing of Fred's plight, he offered to sell his almost-new Plymouth to his uncle. Fred was thrilled. George got a good, fair price for it and was happy to keep on thumbing rides back and forth between Jacksonville and Mayport.

George Jr. adored his Aunt Bessie, a loving, compassionate, wonderfully wise woman who'd been a huge part of young George's upbringing. Frank Groover Long and George Newton Cahill were only a few years apart in age. They were thick as thieves and, as kids, had done everything young boys do together, referring to each other in the shorthand of close cousins as "F.G." and "G.N."

When George Sr. hosted his children during the summers, on those occasions when he could not afford a beach house, he would bunk the kids with his mother Blanche, or next door at Aunt Bessie's house.

Frank and young George would hitchhike to the beach every day spending all their time swimming and chasing girls. Frank had a bicycle and they'd load a wagon with supplies and tow it along on campouts. There was a favorite spot to camp very near the Jacksonville Zoo and, at night, with all the world asleep, the two boys would stare up at the stars and plan magnificent futures for themselves while listening to the lions roar just yards away.

When Frank eventually joined the Navy, about eight months after George had enlisted, he too had done his basic training at Mayport and, now that George was in the Quartermaster's Office, the two cousins could see each other on regular weekends, usually at the Long's house on Trout River.

One of the many charming things about Aunt Bessie was that she was a powerful influence on all the kids and cousins, pushing everyone to go to church. That she was so widely beloved made it an easy sell — for everyone, that is, except her husband. Fred Sr. had once begrudgingly tried to follow her lead and, on a visit to her church years before, hung up a very nice overcoat just outside the sanctuary. After the service the coat was gone, which so infuriated Fred that he vowed never to go back. And he never did. For many years after, when asked why he didn't go to church, Fred's response was always the same — "They stole my coat!"

But that never swayed Bessie's enthusiasm and she continued to encourage everyone to go. In fact, whenever George Jr. was home from the Navy, he would bow to her influence and join the family in worship. Otherwise, church was not a regular part of George's agenda.

During one Sunday visit with the Longs, after Frank returned from church with George, he asked his cousin, "Hey, G.N., you wanna come in and meet my neighbor?"

"Sure, F.G."

5

Mabel

Mabel Rominger, her sister Helen, and their younger brother Paul Rominger had grown up on their parents' 200 acre farm in West Baden Springs, Indiana, in the south of the state about ten miles outside the town of French Lick. Mabel was born May 16, 1899 and, disliking a farm existence from the first, she set her sights on a bigger life. Helen was 10 years younger, born on Thanksgiving Day, November 25, 1909. Making ends meet outside his farm, the 1910 Census lists Everett's profession as Street Car Conductor. He also occasionally served in the fire department.

Academic records indicate Mabel was exceptionally smart and during her time in high school from 1915 to early 1919 she held an after school job as a chambermaid at the nearby West Baden Springs Hotel. Her relationship with her father Everett Perry Rominger was never stable. Everett was a tough farm hand and never gave much care to the niceties in life. There was always work to be done.

Mabel and her younger sister Helen were much closer to their mother, Cena Bostock Rominger. The girls can't have been happy when, sometime in 1914, Cena left Everett and filed for divorce. Though he had loved Cena very much, sometime over the next three years Everett took up with a woman named Mary Harris and made her his wife on May 14, 1918. Mary brought with her to the marriage a daughter, Ruth, from a previous relationship. Then together Everett and Mary had another son, George Rominger, and then two more daughters, Gaithel and Anna Rominger.

It was the summer before Mabel's senior year of high school that she and Helen lost their mother. On July 8, 1918 Cena passed away from unknown causes, just 19 days shy of her 38th birthday.

The next year, after Mabel graduated high school, Everett paid to send her off to Teachers College about 100 miles away in Evansville. But that didn't hold her and, after about a year, Mabel left school and wound up in Memphis, Tennessee.

The 1920 U.S. Census recorded that Mabel Rominger was at that time a boarder in the house of Benjamin and Mollie Hanover at 1010 Galloway Avenue in Ward 19 of Memphis, Tennessee and her job was listed as "Clerk in a Mercantile Agency", her age noted as 20, and her status "Single". About this time she adopted the middle name of Evelyn and occasionally went by the name by "Eve".

It was later put forth by Mabel that her first marriage was to a Roger Bayhe, who was purported to have hailed from a moneyed family in New Orleans. She had become pregnant sometime around Thanksgiving of 1920 and gave birth to a son, Jean Bayhe, on September 22, 1921 in Memphis, Tennessee when she was 22.

Mabel asserted that her husband Roger had been killed in a car crash before Jean was born, although no records have ever been discovered to support this and nothing is known of Mr. Bayhe other than his name. Throughout his life, Jean himself was never convinced that his birth was legitimate and always suspected the purported marriage, as well as Roger's death, and perhaps even Roger himself, may well have been invented. Other than Mabel's say so, no evidence to support or refute any of these suspicions has ever been brought to light.

Mabel's next few years were not well recorded but were likely spent trying to make her way in show business as a single mother, sometimes performing under the stage name Eve Rominger. A 1923 city directory lists her as *Mrs. Mabel Rominger, 870 N. Dunlap Ave. Memphis, TN.* She eventually formed an attachment to a fairly well established actor named Francis H. Sayles who had his own popular touring company in the tradition of American Vaudeville, named appropriately The Francis Sayles Players.

Frank, as he was known to his friends, had been garnering good reviews in all the national theatrical publications dating as far back as 1913. He became so enamored of Mabel that in 1925 he married her, though again an actual marriage license has yet to be discovered.

In Shelby County Tennessee on April 27, 1925 Francis also went so far as to adopt Jean, presumably not long after the marriage. A court order shows a petition was granted to change the three-year-old's name from Jean Bayhe to Francis Harvey Sayles Jr. — Frank perhaps seeing Jean as a surrogate progeny to carry on his own family name. As has long been common in the case of adoptions, an "amended" birth certificate was then issued for Jean inscribed with his new name and, although his family would forever continue to call him Jean, Mabel's son would henceforth be hailed by friends and coworkers as Frank.

Within the next year Francis Sayles was back on the road with his stock company as he continued touring theatres throughout 1926, all the while sending a number of passionate letters and cablegrams to Mabel asking, in fact begging her to join him. Whether she remained behind to establish more stability for herself and Jean, or whether she had perhaps outgrown the relationship altogether, her reasoning was never made clear. But on September 8th 1926, Francis Sayles sent one last impassioned cablegram to Mabel in Memphis from the Auditorium Theatre in Durham, North Carolina. In it he issued this final ultimatum:

"I'm ashamed of you — Your treatment of me has been disgraceful first by you[r] absolute neglect in not answering letters and wires and now by cause for your dismissal — Judging from [your] letter you must have been drunk when it was written — Here is my ultimatum — You will leave there Saturday for here or I am through — No excuse accepted — This is

not a request it is a command — I love you better than anything in the world and trust you but I do not propose to have my peace of mind entirely destroyed — I want you — Need you and it is up to you — If you don't answer immediately I will understand and say God bless you and I shall love you always — Frank."

It is not known whether she replied or if Frank was ever in contact with Mabel or Jean again. However, this cablegram must have been significant in that Mabel would hang onto it for the rest of her life.

Francis H. Sayles eventually gravitated to Los Angeles to make his mark on the big screen. His first known film appearance was playing the bit part of Roberts in a Zasu Pitts oddball murder mystery titled "Strangers of the Evening." The film was released in May of 1932 and thus began Francis Sayles' Hollywood career as a perennial bit player — clerk or cab driver here, bartender or elevator operator there. Over the next twelve years he made appearances in such well known films as "Dodge City" with Errol Flynn, "Ball of Fire" with Gary Cooper, "Blonde Venus" with Marlene Dietrich, "Pride of the Yankees" with Gary Cooper, as well as the classic "Citizen Kane".

Of the 114 films in which Francis H. Sayles acted, all but about a dozen of his appearances are uncredited. He died March 19, 1944 from an unknown ailment while filming "Casanova Brown", again playing opposite Gary Cooper. The film was released six months later.

He was 52.

Within a year or so of Francis Sayles' departure, around 1927 or 1928, Mabel took up with another stage performer and theatrical writer/producer named Charles Kramer. Charlie managed a stock company named, predictably, The Charles Kramer Players, which toured predominantly throughout the south. As Jean had never known a real father figure, he attached himself to Charlie, finding him to be enjoyable company and a companionable enough fellow. Years later

Mary Lou recalled her mother's recollection of him, saying Charlie "had the most pleasant disposition of anyone she ever knew."

With the likelihood that The Charles Kramer Players, with whom Mabel was now a featured performer, was doing well enough financially, she elected to enroll Jean in the Junior Military Academy in Bluefield, West Virginia, an institution with a motto that boasted: "Making Men of Small Boys". At the time they deposited Jean at the academy Mabel was pregnant and, just seven weeks after dropping him off, she gave birth to Mary Luisa Sayles Bayhe Kramer (known as "Mary Lou"), born July 30, 1929 in Asheville, North Carolina, presumably while the company was touring.

Only a few months later the Wall Street stock market crash blindsided the nation.

In the summer of 1930, when the entire country was reeling from the full effect of the Great Depression, Mabel could no longer afford private school for Jean and was sent an invoice from the Junior Military Academy requesting payment for Jean's past due tuition plus room and board for the period from June 5, 1929 to July 7, 1930. Jean would always vividly recall being placed on a train by school officials in the middle of the night and being sent back to his mother. Whatever education he might continue with would have to be found on the road with his family. Jean would often recount how the next few years of being mostly a "street urchin" colored his view of life in a show business family, having to be on his own most days and evenings while his parents plied their trade from town to town.

Mabel and Charlie had no qualms about incorporating the kids in their stage shows as needed. One performance called for an infant in a bassinet and, as Jean recalled later, right in the middle of a scene, his sister's little feet went up, her tiny hands playing with her toes. As she started cooing, the audience erupted with laughter. Of course Mary Lou had no memory of this but Jean often recounted the incident to her with delight.

As a big brother, Jean became Mary Lou's staunch protector, champion, all around caregiver and best friend, looking out for her at every turn throughout the family's tumultuous gypsy life on the road.

Mary Lou was unabashedly vocal from the first. During one of her parents' shows, the toddler would recognize a favorite acquaintance and call out from the audience, "Oh, it's Uncle Al! — Hi, Uncle Al!" After the show the actor would come off stage and sweetly ask her, "Please don't do that."

Very little of the children's life was footlights and frolic. Too many of Mary Lou's earliest memories included waking up to a house filled with passed out, hungover show people who had partied well into another dawn. The youngster became practiced at shaking them awake and asking them to go home.

The 1930's had become exceedingly difficult for everyone, but especially so for itinerant show people. When local audiences couldn't afford the price of admission and Charlie Kramer's stock company couldn't pay its bills, the local sheriff would occasionally close them down and seize their sets and costumes until they could settle accounts. At last Mabel could no longer sustain her family on the road and thus another relationship disassembled itself.

Mary Lou recalled that, "During the depression there was no money and the shows weren't popular any more so my parents went their separate ways." Charlie Kramer had departed for points west before Mary Lou turned two. As such, she had no real memory of her father. But Jean always remembered having liked Charlie quite a bit and was sad to see him go.

It is unclear how many times Mabel took a husband, though it's suspected to be around four. Despite Francis Sayles' binding declaration on Jean's adoption papers that he had indeed married Mabel in 1925, certificates of marriage for her have never been discovered, so there remains some doubt as to how many of her unions (or dissolutions) were ever made legal.

Even after Charlie departed some time in 1931, Mabel would continue to switch between last names of Sayles, Bayhe and Rominger as the occasion suited.

Eventually, succumbing to the pressures of raising two children on her own in the midst of a national Depression, Mabel swallowed her pride and, in late Spring of 1934, returned to the family farm in West Baden Springs, Indiana. Imposing on her family to see after her children for the summer had to have been something of a humiliation. It had gotten so tough that she was unable to care for them as a single mother while the entire country was unemployed. At least on a farm they would never want for food and a place to sleep. And it would give Mabel and Helen a chance to get back on their feet. At the farm Jean stayed with Everett and Mary while Mary Lou stayed in a house on the property with Mabel's brother Paul and his wife Grace.

At summer's end, Mabel returned to collect her children but it is thought that Everett persuaded her to allow Jean to remain in Indiana since he loved being a farm hand and there was a local school he could attend. Whatever the circumstances that prompted the decision, Jean remained and Mabel returned to Florida with Mary Lou. Everett enrolled Jean in 6th grade at Kingdom School #2, the community's one-room school house where Lillian Pruitt was the single teacher for 20 children. In that one room Miss Pruitt simultaneously taught grades 1-through-8.

Whenever he wasn't in school, Jean was always working the farm and, not having a father of his own, the boy was utterly invigorated by working with his grandfather and uncle in the fields.

Jean returned again to Kingdom School for 7th grade under teacher Reid Southern. Mary Lou recalled visiting the Rominger farm and her beloved big brother for the summer of 1936. This time Mary Lou stayed at summer's end and briefly attended school along with Jean. Jean would sit in the back row at school learning with the other

8th graders while little Mary Lou started school in the front row at Kingdom School #2 as a 1st grader.

When Mabel finally arrived in October to take her daughter back to Florida, Mary Lou was thrilled to be going home and happy to finish 1st grade at Gesu Catholic School in Miami.

Mary Lou returned to the Rominger farm the following summer, freeing her mother and Helen for a few months to get ahead financially, but the seven-year-old was extremely unhappy there. She quite disliked life on her grandparents' acreage whereas her big brother took to it so easily and seemed to thrive on outdoor activity and hard work. Plus, having consistent male role models in his life was something new and exciting for the boy. Everett was especially pleased to have Jean around and looked forward to grooming him for the life of a farmer.

During Jean and Mary Lou's time in Indiana, it is unknown how often Mabel put in an appearance, other than the summer exchanges. It is reasonable to presume she at least kept in touch with the Romingers enough to follow the children's progress and hopefully even visited.

When the summer of 1937 ended and Mabel did not appear to collect Mary Lou, Paul and Grace were left with no recourse other than to send her back to school, this time at a larger school in nearby Paoli, Indiana. However, unwilling to lay out the purchase price of new 2nd grade books for Mary Lou, her Uncle Paul re-enrolled her in 1st grade and had her reuse the same books from her previous year.

It wasn't very long into the school year when Mabel discovered, not only that Mary Lou was unnecessarily repeating 1st grade, but — more to her horror — that Jean was not in school at all. The Romingers intended for Jean's education to go no further since, as a farmer, he'd already learned everything he would need to know.

When Mabel discovered Everett had no intention of allowing Jean to go on to high school, she raced back to Indiana. The moment she arrived Mabel engaged her father in a furious fight over her son's future.

She would be taking the children back to Florida to continue their proper schooling.

Jean recalled trying to intervene on his own behalf at the height of the confrontation, confirming that he would much prefer to stay on the farm, at which point Mabel popped him on the head and told him not to get involved.

Everett was firm, even adamant, that Jean would be remaining on the farm. He felt he understood the boy better than Mabel ever would and knew that Jean loved farming. Why would she interfere with that?

This only enraged her and the argument quickly turned into an ugly shouting match that concluded with a searing threat from Mabel — if Everett tried in any way to keep Jean on the farm, she would *kill* him!

Witnesses to this terrifying exchange — Jean, Mary, Paul and Gaithel — were duly unnerved, as was Everett, who honestly believed that, if sufficiently provoked, Mabel was indeed capable of making good on her threat. Many times over the years, both Mary and Gaithel would recount this incident in great detail to Jean's family, adding that, that night after the fight, Everett abandoned his bedroom on the first floor of the farmhouse and, along with his wife, spent the night in an upstairs bedroom where he actually "slept with a gun under his bed."

The next morning, Mabel disappeared with both her children. Everett and Mary were profoundly sad to have lost Jean, whom they'd come to love over the past few years.

Many years later, Jean would often tell his wife and children that, leaving the farm that October day in 1937, was one of the very saddest days of his entire life.

Now settled in Florida, Mabel and Helen alternately held addresses on Miami Beach and a few miles away in Coral Gables. Mary Lou finished 2nd grade, this time in a public school. She loved her mother but was always conflicted about Mabel's short temper and sudden furies. Of course Helen was always around no matter where the winds of fate carried Mabel. A somewhat more sedate version of her big sister, Helen was always a pacifying influence in the children's lives. She and Mabel would fight, make up with, and support each other over the years through the best and the worst of times.

As for Jean, Mary Lou was incredibly close to him; he was the only reliably calm and caring constant in her life. When she was with her big brother, the two of them were inseparable. And when the Depression was beating the family down, the children relied more than ever on each other.

Mabel landed somewhat erratic employment around the Miami area where, among other things, she ran a flower shop for a time, was a paid caregiver, a seamstress, and a sometime voice actor on radio soap operas.

Mabel's children never really knew a father growing up and whenever Mary Lou would ask about her birth father it was intimated by Mabel that Charlie was dead. Then Helen would tell her, "No, I believe he's still alive and I think he's in the military." No one had any true idea of Charlie Kramer's whereabouts and, after a few years, Mary Lou finally stopped asking.

Helen drifted into and out of several romances and marriages of her own over the years, but always ended up, one way or another, partnering up with her sister, through the thick and the thin of it. And though tough times called for tough measures, Mabel managed to muscle through the depression, usually with Helen at her side, pulling off whatever creative feats she could manage to keep the family alive and, frequently, on the move. When they did have a place to stay Mary Lou was often asked to answer the door and lie to bill collectors saying her mother wasn't home.

There were long stretches while Mabel was working, usually out of town, when she boarded Mary Lou and Jean, though not always together. Sometimes the children stayed with their Aunt Helen and sometimes at a boarding school where the food was terrible, but more frequently it was with local families, and often for weeks at a time. Little Mary Lou loved the occasional weekend when her mother came to visit and they could be together.

In one instance in particular a young couple with whom Mary Lou was staying had developed such affection for this sweet little girl that they made a sincere offer to adopt her. Upon hearing this, Mabel raced right over and snatched her away, removing any possibility of breaking up their family.

When the chips were down, Mabel invariably did whatever was required. There were times Mary Lou recalled her mother having to bargain with a lunch counter attendant so the two of them could get a plate of spaghetti "on the cuff" until payday.

"She always provided", recalled Mary Lou. "She never had any money. And I always felt she should have spent more on herself. She went without to make sure I looked pretty and had nice clothes."

As Mary Lou approached her teenage years, she was made by Mabel to dress more like a grown up than was common for a girl her age. While every other girl at school was still in saddle shoes, bobby socks and sweaters, Mary Lou for the most part had begun to move on to dresses, nylons and pumps. Her mother very much wanted her daughter to be taken seriously, and seriously she was very much taken.

Mary Lou was an incredibly smart and savvy girl who knew a lot for one so young. Having traveled widely and spent her formative years in the company of gregarious theatre people, as well as under the strong influence of two strong willed women, she accelerated past many of the fumblings of early girlhood to arrive at a brand of quick witted confidence that only comes from being comfortable in one's own skin.

Managing to survive her mother's frequent pendulum swings from poverty to excess and back again had given Mary Lou a worldliness beyond her years, yet never jading or compromising her innate innocence. Though she benefitted from her mother's and aunt's examples of confident stage presence, she never shared their hunger for the spotlight. Mary Lou's own dreams were modest.

However nomadic her existence may have been, there was a fiery brilliance somewhere inside Mabel that came out in a powerful drive to be creative. Mary Lou inherited a good portion of that creativity and, years later, for children of her own, she would sew inventive Halloween costumes and, wherever she lived, she appointed her surroundings with a style that outshone their economy, always decorating with zest for holidays and other celebrations. In the tradition of her own talented mother, Mary Lou developed into a first rate cook, inspired decorator and avid gardener, turning every home into a showplace.

Mabel wanted the very best education for Mary Lou and, even though she herself was not religious, Catholic schools had a reputation for exceptional academic and moral standards. They were also expensive. And though Mabel somehow managed it for a short time, she could not maintain the exorbitant fees. She had enrolled Mary Lou in parochial school for 3rd grade and, sometime during fourth grade, Mabel was preparing to take her out of Catholic school when the priest who was the Principal asked why.

"I can't afford it any more."

He jumped to her daughter's defense. "Don't do it. We'll work something out."

And he did.

He agreed to waive all tuition and fees if she would leave Mary Lou in Catholic school. It was clear she was thriving there like no place else she'd ever been. That same year Mary Lou was baptized a Catholic and took her first communion. Two years later in 6th grade she was confirmed Catholic.

On a bright Sunday afternoon in 1941, while walking home from the movies, Mary Lou was startled by people in the streets shouting, "WAR! We're at WAR!" The Japanese had bombed pearl harbor.

For the children, the news was alarming but changed little for them. Living in Coral Gables, Jean held 2 jobs — a paper route in the mornings, and after school he delivered telegrams. He also played tuba in the band at school and ended up graduating 2nd in his Class from Ponce de Leon High School in 1942. He then headed off to the Massachusetts Institute of Technology (MIT) in Boston to study engineering.

As Mary Lou was too young to do anything else, she volunteered as a "plane spotter" on Saturdays. Radar would not become widely available until late 1944 so visual sightings were the only method of tracking enemy planes. During the week after school, she'd spend most afternoons at the Duval County Rationing Board helping distribute rationed goods such as sugar, meat, shortening and butter. Two afternoons a week Mary Lou was a nurse's aide at St. Vincent's Hospital in Riverside.

That October, after Jean had gone to Boston, Mabel packed up her daughter and moved to Jacksonville, Florida to be closer to her sister Helen and where Mary Lou entered 7th grade at St. Joseph's Academy. Jean of course could not sit out the war and, in 1943, he broke off his studies at MIT to join the U.S. Army.

Helen Rominger Miller was known by her Jacksonville neighbors as a beautiful woman who had a lovely house next door to Frank and Bessie Long. She'd been married a number of times, once to a county sheriff who had passed away some years before. You could tell she came from show business and carried herself with a well tempered dignity and easy grace. She had a shimmering drape of honey blonde hair that, when not wrapped up behind her slender neck, fell down in streams long enough to sit on. But her beauty wasn't merely physical. Helen was attractive in the way that people of confidence seemed to be.

Helen's older sister Mabel was equally striking, what many would call a classic beauty. It was known that both women hailed from years on the stage but the 1930's had turned their fortunes. They'd only just made it through the Depression by the skin of their teeth and, though Mabel was still struggling, Helen seemed lately to have landed on more solid ground, enough to maintain a house on Trout River left to her by her late husband.

At the time Mabel was renovating an old country farm house of her own that she'd bought from a dentist. The house was in Mandarin about 18 miles outside Jacksonville. Mabel was good at making the most of any bad situation and had a long history of spinning suffering into silver. Whatever the undertaking, she devoted herself to it wholeheartedly and with gusto. Yet behind all that enthusiasm, she was not demonstrably affectionate. Nonetheless, Mary Lou occasionally glimpsed a mother's devotion seeping through.

"She never said, 'I love you' that I can remember. But she did say, 'I wouldn't be strict with you if I didn't care about you. I wouldn't be as hard on you as I am.'"

And that was good enough for Mary Lou.

She had turned 13 in the summer of 1942. And yet, to look at her, to see her carry herself and converse with others, it was easy to observe a clear sophistication. Fashion and personal presentation were high on Mabel and Helen's list of priorities and they passed that strong sense of style on to Mary Lou, who, as a youngster, had spent endless hours mooning over starlets in movie magazines and drawing her own fashion designs for paper dolls. Mabel was an incredibly strict mother but never treated Mary Lou like a child who, at an early age, had already acquired an abundance of something not many grown women, and fewer girls, would ever possess — poise.

She was also a quick study.

On the 18 mile drive home one day from Jacksonville to their little farmhouse Mary Lou made a purely casual remark that it must be nice to know how to drive a car. Her mother spontaneously pulled over and put Mary Lou in the driver's seat. After a few basic instructions about gearshift, clutch and gas, this 13-year-old girl not only drove home that day, but thereafter would take the car by herself into the city with no grief from her mother. Mabel encouraged her daughter to be not a girl, but a responsible young woman, something at which she seemed to excel. And being raised by a couple of canny show business dames, Mary Lou exhibited no bashful tendencies. She was comfortably forthright with everyone she met.

Her friends at school, especially her best friend Margaret Haugdaul, knew from the first that, with Mary Lou, they were in the company of a grownup. Having lived in so many places, Margaret considered her friend's life utterly exotic.

"She was sophisticated," Margaret recalled. "All the girls wanted to be her. She dressed, spoke and behaved like a grownup. So elegant. She knew how to drive long before any of us. And yet she was always just one of us, but a much more mature version. She was always mature."

In school Mary Lou was not only an outstanding academic but excelled in every extracurricular activity she could get her hands on like cheerleading, theatrical productions and editing the school newspaper. Mary Lou's strong feelings about pursuing a Catholic education for her own children many years later would be fueled by these incredibly positive experiences.

Catholic school had in fact been the first real and substantial stability she'd experienced in her life. Never had she been so completely nurtured in mind and spirit. It was undoubtedly the most uplifting and enriching foundation Mary Lou might have wished for and, in her heart, a Catholic education would be the wellspring of everything good she was ever to know.

In the Spring of 1943 Mary Lou Sayles was staying with her Aunt Helen at the house next door to the Longs on Trout River. And one bright Sunday afternoon Frank Long knocked on their door.

6

A Ramblin' Wreck

Knowing that the niece of her neighbor Helen Rominger Miller had been baptized, Bessie Long volunteered that, any Sunday she cared to, young Mary Lou was welcome to go to church along with her boys Frank and Jack. And Mary Lou often joined them, at least on as regular a basis as visits would permit. She was already fast friends with the Long boys and they held her in the esteem of a little sister.

In just a few months Mary Lou would be 14 but already she carried herself with quiet assurance. When Frank brought her in from next door, George stood up to meet this bright eyed girl.

She was fair complected with clear blue eyes, a heart shaped face, and wavy shoulder length hair the shade of warm chestnut. She wore a simple blue dress and readily engaged in cheerful conversation. George was all of 20, casually well mannered and looking smart in his Navy blues, standing 6-feet even at a trim 163 pounds. It was a brief encounter that neither George nor Mary Lou would recall as being anything more than pleasantly cordial.

Throughout the rest of the summer, on weekends spent knocking around with Frank, and sometimes with Jack, George and his cousins would occasionally encounter Mary Lou, who spent a lot of time at Bessie's house. They'd exchange greetings and chat a little, but not much more.

George Sr. was becoming more and more the most popular fixture in Jacksonville, enjoying perks from fellow city employees and business owners. One such perk came in the form of three free tickets to the Ringling Bros./Barnum & Bailey Circus. Unable to use them himself, he offered them to George Jr. who, since Frank was unavailable, offered a second ticket to Jack Long. For the third ticket he thought perhaps Mary Lou Sayles would be interested and young George phoned next door to invite her.

Mary Lou asked her Aunt Helen, who thought it a pleasant idea since she was quite fond of the Longs and had gotten to know George a little and liked him. So, on October 29, 1943, George, Jack Long and Mary Lou Sayles went to the circus. Having never spent so much time in each other's company before, George and Mary Lou began to recognize commonalities. Thereafter, whenever they ran into each other during George's frequent visits, their conversations grew longer and longer.

At the end of one evening at the Long's, George offered to walk Mary Lou home.

"But I'm just going next door," she said.

Nonetheless George walked with her. They talked a little longer and ended up agreeing to write to each other. During the war it was a common practice, and even considered patriotic, to write letters to servicemen. So Mary Lou and George began a companionable correspondence exchanging letters.

Though none of the letters survive, it was indicated they contained only the briefest exchanges; knock-knock jokes, comments on the social scene or the weather, news of mutual friends, and just plain nonsense. Nothing of any gravity or consequence. But enough to stitch together the fabric of a burgeoning relationship.

"We started a correspondence that lasted the rest of the war and all through his college years," recalled Mary Lou. "It got to where I was coming home and finding a letter in the box every day. We got to know each other through those letters."

At the outset of America's entry into World War II, attendance at U.S. colleges had taken a significant nosedive. With the majority of the country's young men who would otherwise be pursuing a degree now suddenly off supporting the war effort, many universities feared having to close their doors for the duration. In reaction to this very real dilemma the American Council on Education[1] published a report in October 1942 proposing that a "college training corps" enroll members of the armed forces in schools across the country. These enlisted men would continue to receive active-duty pay while being trained in technical specialties that would be of use to the Army and Navy.

President Franklin D. Roosevelt agreed and instructed the Secretary of War and Secretary of the Navy to get on board. The result was the Army Specialized Training Program (ASTP) as well as the Navy V-12 Program[2], both jointly announced in December 1942. V-12 had more appeal to the schools involved because the program's students would be permitted to attend school along side civilian students and participate in athletics. Plus, the lion's share of the curriculum was already being taught by civilian instructors.

The idea was to bolster the military's requirement for more technically skilled officers and, by agreeing to go through the V-12 program, candidates would receive a fully paid college education, in exchange for which they would give serious consideration afterward to becoming officers in the U.S. Navy.

V-12 was officially instituted on July 1st 1943. Having thought of himself as only an average student in high school, George harbored doubts whether he would qualify. Becoming an engineer had only ever been a Tom Swiftian pipe dream, but he'd never forgive himself if he didn't at least give it a shot. George and his cousin Frank applied right away and took the qualifying test together.

After one full month of agonizing over the results, both George and Frank were notified of their acceptance into the Navy's V-12

---

1. https://en.wikipedia.org/wiki/American_Council_on_Education

2.   https://en.wikipedia.org/wiki/V-12_Navy_College_Training_Program

program and would begin their respective college careers as Freshmen when the next available semester started in the Fall.

Of all the engineering schools in the country, the closest to Jacksonville was the Georgia Institute of Technology so that's where George elected to go. It also didn't hurt that they had a great football team. Frank, looking for a career in obstetrics, chose to attend Boston University Medical School for his undergraduate studies. Come Fall of 1943, the two cousins would be going their separate ways. At least until they earned their degrees.

The Navy bought George a train ticket up to Georgia Tech and, in preparation for registration, he met with a counselor to sketch out his curriculum. The Navy paid for everything; classes, books, supplies, room and board — even the slide rule required by all engineers to manually work out mathematical calculations, a keepsake he would hang onto for the rest of his life.

Studying engineering at any school, let alone one of the most prestigious technical universities in the country, set the stakes high. One crucial caveat was that the Navy required each man, without exception, to maintain passing grades in all courses. Otherwise, it'd be back to regular naval service and goodbye, degree.

At the Georgia Institute of Technology[3] in 1943 the school's symbol was (and still is) a yellow-jacket bee. But the school mascot, in honor of all the engineers the university produced, was a 1914 Ford affectionately referred to as the "Ramblin' Wreck[4]" (or alternately "Ramblin' Reck"). It was an old Model-T automobile that had been driven to and from school every day by one of the university's most beloved alumnus. This seemingly ramshackle vehicle represented the resourceful integrity of engineers who could keep an otherwise outdated piece of machinery in good working condition with constant ingenuity and care. The rickety mascot put in regular appearances at

---

3. https://en.wikipedia.org/wiki/Georgia_Tech

4. https://en.wikipedia.org/wiki/Ramblin'_Wreck

sporting events and school functions, and George now bore the distinct honor of being yet another "Ramblin' Wreck" from Georgia Tech. Despite so cavalier a label, the stringent academics he faced meant his concentration over the next four years would need to be in top form. He dove in with all his might and worked hard at the difficult curriculum, only occasionally taking a break for relaxation.

The Navy covered George's initial nine-hour train ride to Atlanta to get to school. Getting back and forth thereafter would be his problem. During breaks over the next few years he'd occasionally hitch a ride home with a classmate. But mostly he would purchase a train ticket. On arrival in Jacksonville, Mary Lou started showing up at the station to meet him, which naturally led to them spending more time together. Once or twice Mary Lou went so far as to convince her Aunt Helen to make the five and a half hour one-way drive to pick George up at school and then drive him back after break, but that was rare.

Throughout the 40's dancing was an enormous public preoccupation and the featured highlight of any social occasion. In the winter of 1944 Mary Lou received the gift of a "Bid" (a free pass) to attend the annual Christmas dance at St. Paul's School in nearby Riverside and she asked her mother whether it would be too forward of her to ask George to escort her. Mabel told her that, had she gone out and purchased the tickets herself, then yes, that would be considered forward. But since she received the Bid as a gift, then it was perfectly acceptable for her to ask him to go with her.

She'd never been to a formal dance with a full length gown and was anxious to experience her first. She knew George would be coming home for Christmas break and wrote to him at school asking if he'd like to take her. He wrote back saying he'd be happy to.

As a high school girl, Mary Lou's friends were impressed (but not surprised) that, mostly owing to her maturity, she would be going out with a college man. "But", as Margaret Haugdaul remembered, "she was always much more sophisticated than the rest of us so it seemed appropriate."

George picked up Mary Lou at his cousin Harriet's house where Mary Lou had changed into a lovely taffeta gown. He had bought her a red rose corsage and they both enjoyed the evening very much. A photographer captured them in mid dance at the event, which by all accounts was still not the beginning of any great love affair. Both Mary Lou and George maintained that the relationship at this stage was still very cordial.

It was the 29th of December 1944 and, in the car on the way home from the dance, George asked Mary Lou if she'd like to go see a midnight movie with him. Again she said she'd have to ask her mother but that, yes, she'd like to go. The film was "For Whom the Bell Tolls" starring Gary Cooper and Ingrid Bergman. Mabel and Helen thought it would be all right and gave permission for Mary Lou to go.

According to George, "This was the first real date we went on."

Mary Lou drove her mother's car and parked it outside George's father's house. Then, using his father's car, George drove them both to the Florida Theatre in downtown Jacksonville. After the movie they went to a drive-in BBQ place, had a sandwich and talked a little while. Finally he took Mary Lou back to her mother's car and, as she would be driving 18 miles by herself at such a late hour, he would follow along to see her safely home. By now it was close to 4:00 AM.

About two thirds of the way home they passed Helen's car coming from the opposite direction — it was Mabel out looking for them. And it suddenly hit Mary Lou: "Uh oh, I think I'm in trouble."

As she slowed down, George pulled up next to her car and, with a quick wave and a smile said, "See ya!", pulled a U-turn and was gone.

Once back home Mabel was irate, demanding to know where the two of them had been. Mary Lou calmly laid out the time frame for her — the movie didn't start until midnight and got out at 2:30. Then they stopped for something to eat after which they headed straight home.

Mable finally conceded the times made sense. But this 15-year-old had been out very late, and with a sailor no less. In future, she'd be more exacting about a curfew for her daughter.

George had known from an early age what he most wanted to be and, as recommended by a Georgia Tech guidance counselor, he'd enrolled in all the requisite courses for a degree in Civil Engineering. College proved a considerable challenge and George recalled his second year roommate being a young man named Alfred M. Bork who also hailed from Jacksonville. They were assigned to the same room in Techwood Dorm and spent a good deal of their time in an adjacent study room that they shared with two other students.

Alfred Bork was known on campus as "The Brain" as he had a reputation for never ever making a mistake or scoring less than 100% on any test he took. George very fondly remembers him as an excellent tutor with great patience who was eager to assist anyone who asked — and he was asked by practically every student for guidance. As Alfred appeared not to have much of a social life, he studied constantly and delighted in keeping up on all the latest developments in mathematics. George especially relied on him for assistance and the fellow was always happy to drop what he was doing to help deconstruct a problem. The complexities of engineering just came naturally to Mr. Bork.

"He was the smartest guy I've ever known. And that's saying a lot."

George attributes a good portion of his success at Georgia Tech to Alfred who was so accomplished that, in his Senior year, he was asked by the faculty to teach an advanced math class.

Though he and George never saw each other after graduation, Alfred M. Bork would go on, not only to earn a commission in the U.S. Navy, but to some degree of fame in the world of engineering, especially in what was then the very young field of computers. He would later pioneer many of the advanced theories in computer-based learning for science and mathematics. He was a vocal proponent of utilizing personal computers as integral tools for simplifying technical education.

After Georgia Tech Alfred Bork took advanced degrees in Physics at Brown University. Then taught at Reed University for several years and finally landed a tenured position as Physics professor at University of California, Irvine. As he clearly had a knack for it, the man spent his life joyfully teaching math and physics. Students from his early years of teaching in the 1970's recalled him (in his wild pink pants and green shoes) employing delightfully unorthodox classroom methods to get the very best work from them. He authored four books on using personal computers for education. A much beloved professor, friend and brainy good guy, Alfred Morton Bork passed away in 2007 survived by his wife of almost 60 years and three daughters.

George would always remember with great fondness the quirky "brain" who gently guided him through his early university studies.

The Navy required sailors to maintain an official dress code, even, and especially, while they were in college. Per regulation, the men sported their classic blue uniforms in winter and wore the whites in summer.

Strangely, the powers that be had also come up with a dress uniform specifically designed for students enrolled in the V-12 program. It consisted of navy dress slacks, white shirt, navy tie and a brass buttoned navy dress tunic, topped off with a black-billed white hat, and all trimmed up with the program's own unique insignia.

The V-12 uniform confused a lot of people because it looked remarkably like a naval officer's uniform. No one could quite explain why and, amusingly, George was never tempted to correct anyone who treated him as an officer. With the V-12 program initially intended to cultivate new officers, the thinking higher up may well have been to present these young men in the guise of an officer so that, once graduated, perhaps they'd be inclined to actually become one. However, once the war was over, little incentive remained to lure very many V-12 graduates with a commission. Neither George nor Frank would pursue becoming an officer.

While World War II was still being fought, the Department of Labor estimated that, after the war, 15 million men and women who had been serving in the armed forces would be unemployed. To reduce the possibility of postwar depression brought on by widespread unemployment, the National Resources Planning Board, a White House agency, started studying postwar manpower needs as early as 1942, and in June 1943 recommended a series of programs for education and training. The American Legion designed the main features of what became the Serviceman's Readjustment Act and pushed it through Congress. The bill, often referred to as the G.I. Bill of Rights[5], unanimously passed both chambers of Congress in spring of 1944. President Franklin D. Roosevelt signed it into law on June 22, 1944, just days after the D-day invasion of Normandy.

On June 25, 1946 Quartermaster 3rd Class George Newton Cahill Jr. was honorably discharged from military service, having served three years, eight months and five days with the United States Navy. With the end of his service also came the conclusion of his participation in the V-12 Program, at which time he was able to rely on the G.I. Bill of Rights to subsidize the completion of his degree at Georgia Tech.

His cousin Frank Long had left high school early to join the Navy. The V-12 Program had given him entrée to MIT and he later transferred to Tufts University in Boston. After graduating, he went to Temple University's Medical School in Philadelphia where he met Mary Hiloski, who was in nursing school. The two would later be married in Philadelphia.

---

5.   https://en.wikipedia.org/wiki/G.I._Bill

The house where Flo, Sandy and George Sr. lived at 783 Old Hickory Road in Jacksonville was always full of people, especially on weekends when they all listened to the fights on the radio. Still, they were happy to make room for one more when, just one week shy of little Sandy's 7th birthday, Flo gave birth to Lawrence Ernest Cahill ("Larry") on the 11th of September 1946.

George Jr. remembered babysitting Sandy while their new brother was being delivered. Yet, finding time alone with his father was at more and more of a premium.

As the man in charge of handing out permits for every single business in Jacksonville, George Sr. was widely popular. He had a great number of amiable relationships with the city's business leaders and politicians, many of whom were frequent visitors to his home. He threw plenty of parties and hosted a regular card game at his house practically every Saturday.

These gatherings were populated by local gentry, sports and political figures, and even the mayor. Often in attendance, Mary Lou was an active contributor to those vibrant conversations and was entirely comfortable being on an equal footing with George Sr.'s business acquaintances and poker pals, many of whom treated her almost as one of the boys.

A boyfriend of Aunt Helen's was a county sheriff who had previously passed along to Mary Lou an avid interest in social, political and civic responsibility as well as world events. As a seasoned show biz kid, she easily held her own in energetic discussions of local politics and other hot button issues typically reserved for billiard parlors and board rooms.

Her easygoing demeanor seemed to follow more closely the temperament of her Aunt Helen rather than the high octane personality of her mother. For a young woman who naturally put people at ease with a pleasant wit and exceptional mind, Mary Lou was the hit of any room she chose to enter. And all without the slightest notion that anyone in that room was more or less important than she.

In 1947, home from his Junior year, George Jr. went looking for a summer job. On his behalf, George Sr. had reached out to several people he knew at a radio station and other local businesses. One interview was at an engineering firm, which at the time had no openings. But not long afterwards, Allied Chemical Corporation approached that same company about building a new plant for them in Jacksonville. The firm had remembered George and called him back, saying Allied needed someone just for the summer to be on site to babysit construction of the new facility — was he interested? John B. Sundy, Allied's supervisor in charge of the installation process, interviewed George and decided to bring him on board.

Being an out of towner, John Sundy needed to open a business account for the new plant out on Picketville Road and went to the bank with George to set it up. Since the bank's Vice President knew George Sr., the man readily conceded that Mr. Sundy, as an associate of George Jr., could "have all the credit you want." John Sundy was immediately impressed.

During construction George wasn't satisfied to merely babysit the operation. He asked questions of the construction team, probing and investigating how everything was intended to work once the finished plant was up and running. He followed every step in great detail. Mr. Sundy would swing by once a month or more to see how things were progressing. So impressed was he with George's acquired knowledge of the construction, and with his diligent reports on the developing process, he recognized right away this kid was no mere babysitter. Upon his return to Allied headquarters in New York, he offered up George's name as an ideal, self-starting future employee.

The Jacksonville plant had been designed to manufacture aluminum sulfate, a water purification agent. The substance was primarily employed when an industrial operation relied on water from a local source such as a river. Any impurities in the untreated water would first have to be excised so as not to contaminate the manufacturing process. Aluminum sulfate is added to the source water, often in a pond or holding tank, in order to coagulate and separate mud particulates and other impurities, allowing the clarified portion to be siphoned off. Aluminum sulfate was a crucial ingredient for any business in which its processes used a lot of water, such as in steel and paper mills. This new plant was specifically designed to be a one-man operation. But that one man would really have to know what he was doing.

Through her Junior and Senior years at St. Joseph's Academy Mary Lou had an after school job at Purcell's, a high end women's apparel store in downtown Jacksonville. In addition to this job, and while maintaining good marks in her studies, Mary Lou served as editor of the school yearbook, sold tickets to every school event, performed in all the plays, served as a popular football and basketball cheerleader (known as "Legs Sayles" — not only because she had great legs but she also had a truly impressive high-kick), and was even elected Senior Class President.

After graduating from St. Joseph's, Mary Lou was hired to work for the Duval Board of Public Instruction starting as a file clerk and later a secretary. She was quite well liked by the two women who ran it and proved something of an asset to the organization.

In the Spring of 1947 George told his father he intended to marry Mary Lou. George Sr. got along famously with his daughter-in-law to be and both he and Flo embraced the idea completely. George then told Frank and also his mother, who of course adored Mary Lou and heartily approved. He then informed his sister Mary who told Don.

And finally he told Frank's older brother Fred, whose wife promptly gave George a superb piece of advice for his marriage — "Never go to bed mad."

A few weeks before the end of Spring semester, and just prior to the summer break before his final year of school, Allied Chemical headquarters sent a representative to Georgia Tech to gage George's interest in taking over supervision of the new Jacksonville plant once he graduated.

"Absolutely, I'll take it."

With a college degree one year away and a solid job offer under his belt, George felt the timing would never be more right. The next week Mary Lou was to complete her studies at St. Joesph's Academy and, the day before she graduated, he went with her to Jacksonville beach where they spent a marvelous day. When he drove her home to Mandarin, before she got out, there in his father's car parked in front of her mother's house, George produced a ring and proposed to Mary Lou.

It was Thursday, May 31st, 1947.

Ever so briefly Mary Lou hesitated, but immediately realized if she didn't say yes, some other woman would get him. And of course, she loved him. More than she'd realized. More than either of them had known.

The answer was yes.

The one caveat — he had to first ask her mother's permission.

To George, Mabel Rominger was "a tough customer" and he was a little intimidated by her. He had asked Mabel's blessing while she was preparing dinner, and it didn't help that she was holding a large kitchen knife the whole time.

At first Mabel suggested that perhaps her daughter ought to go to college before marrying. But Mary Lou countered that, "There was nothing I wanted to be — nothing I wanted to study to learn to be."

What she wanted was to get married and raise a family. And George was the one she wanted to do that with. In the end her mother conceded that Mary Lou knew her own mind and that it would work out well. She also knew George was good for her daughter. Mabel gave her consent, but with a single firm condition — "No divorce!"

Later, when George shared with Mary Lou the advice from Fred Long's wife about never going to be mad, she immediately adopted it as words to live by. Both Mary Lou and George concurred that, whatever the disagreement, they would always make up with each other before going to sleep. This advice served them well. As George recalled, "It was one of the few secrets that made for a successful marriage.

George and his dad were closer than ever and it was quite something when he asked his father to be his best man. George Sr. was bursting with pride over his soon-to-be college graduate son whose future of happiness was all but guaranteed. And he adored Mary Lou. She also thought the world of her father-in-law to be. According to her, he was an incredibly personable fellow who always had a smile and a great story to tell.

"He was a real gentleman and never went to answer the door without his coat on", she would say with a bit of an Irish lilt. "That's an Irish thing, don't ya know. You never go to the door without your coat."

Back at school George buckled down on all his studies to finish out his degree in earnest. And Mary Lou got busy planning the wedding. She was saving every cent from her job at the Jacksonville School Board.

One time George came home on the train for the weekend and, unbeknownst to Mary Lou, he showed up across the street from her job at quitting time to surprise her. As she came out the front door, she lost her footing and tumbled down the half dozen or so marble steps to the sidewalk. George dashed across the street and, though she wasn't very much hurt, and more than a little embarrassed, she was very surprised that it was her own fiancé appearing out of nowhere to help her to her feet.

It would not be the last time he'd be there for her when she needed him most.

They agreed that George's full attention was to be on school and graduation. Nothing was to rob his focus and everything about the wedding would be left entirely in her hands. Mary Lou talked at length with her best friend Margaret Haugdaul about wedding guests, bridesmaids, dresses, music and refreshments. She worked out every detail and found every possible bargain to put together the loveliest event on a minuscule budget. Her own father had left when she was two and she had no memory of the man. And her mother had never had any money. So this enterprising youngster was footing the bill for the entire affair by herself. The dress would be the biggest budget item, but it would still have to be a stunner. Of course, forget feeding everyone a full meal.

"Who can afford that?", she declared.

Guests would have to be happy with a bowl of punch and a slice of cake. A local hall could be rented for the reception, a modest fee for a small combo of musicians to provide reception music, and token honorariums to the priest conducting the ceremony as well as the organist. A few dollars for invitations and postage would certainly be sufficient. The entire event was cobbled together with military precision at an out-of-pocket cost to Mary Lou of about $1000.00, not at all an insignificant sum in for an 18-year-old girl to raise by herself in 1948.

It was to be a June wedding.

George Sr. and Flo Cahill loved celebrations, especially dancing. They were great aficionados of live music and were certain to be the hit of any dance floor they set foot on. George Sr. however had suffered for some time from a bad stomach ulcer. It became so severe as to require an operation and Mary Lou visited him in the hospital during his recovery the second week of April 1948.

"I would bring him magazines and he would ask me again and again, 'Now, when you're married, you're not going to tie George to your apron strings, are you? You're going to let him go out once a week to be with the boys, right?'"

Mary Lou assured him that his son would be no prisoner. And then he'd ask how the preparations were going and they'd talk about how much he was looking forward to the wedding.

Once out of the hospital, George Sr. was to spend some weeks recovering. But after only a few days at home he couldn't resist the itch and he and Flo went out dancing. A couple of days later, he was feeling unwell and on Sunday April 18th he checked back into St. Luke's hospital. Likely owing to the some undetermined missteps during his surgery — that, in combination with too much activity too soon after the procedure — George Sr.'s stitches had broken loose, triggering a massive internal infection. By the time the problem was discovered the infection had taken too great a hold.

It fell on Mary Lou to call George at college to tell him his father had died. He had languished for five days and expired at 8:32 AM on Thursday April 22nd 1948. He'd celebrated his 49th birthday just six weeks earlier. And yet, in so many ways, he had still been a very young man.

Frank Long would later review the medical records of George Sr.'s operation and conclude the surgery "had not been done properly at all". But there was really nothing more to be done.

The entire city of Jacksonville deeply mourned the passing of George Newton Cahill Sr. The Duval County Tax Office where he'd worked in the City Courthouse was closed in his honor the day of his funeral and the service was attended by almost 2000 people paying their respects, including a number of city officials and the county sheriff. The entire event required a number of police escorts to manage the traffic.

George had held his father in the highest measure of esteem and affection. "He was a great person. A really great person. He was, I won't say my idol, but the model of what I wanted to be; not the career person, but the *man*. He was one of the kind of people you remember all your life once you've met him and talked to him and associated with him. And it wasn't just with me. He was the most popular person I've ever known."

After the funeral George returned to college to complete his final exams and prepare for the graduation his father had so looked forward to.

Throughout his time at Georgia Tech the university sponsored a number of dances at local churches. These were well attended affairs, often with live music, where young people arrived in droves to dance with college students and men in uniform. There was no shortage of young women who found a lot to desire in any young man about to graduate college and set off on a good career. George had accompanied his classmates throughout the year, socializing and dancing at such get togethers, but his devotion was to Mary Lou. Georgia Tech's own Senior dance in 1948 hosted the Jimmy Dorsey orchestra and George proudly escorted his fiancé.

George Newton Cahill Jr. graduated from Georgia Tech with a Bachelor's Degree in Civil Engineering on a muggy Wednesday in Atlanta on June 9th 1948. Four days later back in Jacksonville, George and Mary Lou were married on Sunday June 13th at 6:00 in the evening, dodging the worst heat of the day. Early that morning Mary Lou had gone to church and "prayed to God that I have a long and happy marriage."

George asked his cousin Frank Long to stand up for him as his best man and Frank was honored to accept. The following announcement in the Society section of the Jacksonville Times from Monday June 14, 1948 details some specifics of the wedding that Mary Lou put together. Beneath a formal photo of the newly married couple, was a banner heading, and this two-column report:

Mary Luisa Sayles is Bride
of George Newton Cahill Jr.

Miss Mary Luisa Sayles, daughter of Mrs. Rominger Sayles, and George Newton Cahill Jr., son of Mrs. J.C. Grant of Tampa, and the late George N. Cahill of this city, were united in marriage at 6 o'clock Sunday afternoon, June 13. The double ring ceremony was solemnized by Monsignor D.A. Lyons in St. Paul's Catholic Church.

The church and altar were decorated with lighted white tapers in candelabra and tall baskets of white gladioluses and chrysanthemums. The family pews were marked with lighted tapers and tuberoses.

Prior to the ceremony, a program of nuptial music was rendered by Mrs. Jessie M. Elliott, church organist. The solos were Schubert's "Ave Maria" and "Panis Angelicus" (Cesar Franck). The traditional wedding marches were used.

Acting as best man for the bridegroom was his cousin, Frank T. Long. Don Nutting, Harry Hardwick, Robert J. McFarland, Brothers-in-law of the bridegroom, were ushers.

The bride entered the church on the arm of her brother, F.H. Sayles, who gave her in marriage. Miss Margaret Hougdahl (sp) was maid-of-honor and the bridesmaids were the Misses Marie Shashy, Edith Abraham, Connie Bianco and Pat King. The flower girls were Cheryl Parfitt and Janie Arnold, cousin of the bridegroom.

The bride wore a gown of heavy ivory satin with a sweetheart neckline. The fitted bodice tapered to a point in the back and the long tight sleeves were caught at the wrist with self-covered buttons, forming a point over the hand. The skirt hung in folds, ending in a long train. The full-length, tiered bridal veil of illusion fell from an ivory satin halo. Her bouquet was a spray of tuberoses centered with a white orchid. Her only ornament was a pearl necklace, gift of the bridegroom.

The maid-of-honor and bridesmaids wore identical gowns in pastel shades of marquisette over taffeta, made with a ruffle off-the-shoulder. Their hoop skirts were draped, following the shoulder design. Their old-fashioned picture hats, slippers and mittens matched their dresses. Miss Shashy wore pink; Miss Bianco, green; Miss Abraham, yellow; Miss King, orchid, and Miss Hougdahl, blue. They carried matching nose gays of chrysanthemums.

The flower girls wore pink dresses fashioned after the other attendants. They wore halos of pink roses and carried white arm baskets of rose petals.

The bride's mother wore an original model of grey crepe made on draped lines. Her hat was of matching crepe trimmed with starched veiling. She wore a shoulder corsage of white gardenias.

The bridegroom's mother wore grey crepe with gold and pink accessories. Her hat was of pink flowers with a matching corsage of pink roses.

Following the wedding, a reception was held in the lounge of the Jacksonville Woman's Club. Receiving the guests at the door was Mrs. Helen Miller, aunt of the bride. The receiving line formed in front of the mantle which was decorated with white chrysanthemums and lighted with white tapers. The bride's table was covered with an imported lace cover and centered with a three-tiered bride's cake. On either end of the table were silver candelabra draped with garlands of white chrysanthemums. During the reception, Mrs. Jessie DeVore and a stringed trio played appropriate selections.

Pouring punch were Mrs. Frederick Warren Long, Mrs. George Cahill Sr., Mrs. Don Nutting and Mrs. Robert J. McFarland. Mrs. Harry Hardwick kept the bride's book and Mrs. Parker Henderson cut the cake.

After spending some time with their guests, Mr. and Mrs. Cahill left for a motor trip to Washington, New York and Canada. Mrs. Cahill traveled in a grey suit with burgundy and blue accessories. Her corsage was an orchid.

Mrs. Cahill was born in Asheville, North Carolina, but has spent most of her life in Miami and Jacksonville. She is a graduate of St. Joseph's Academy and is identified with the Alumni group. She is a member of the Catholic Professional Women's Club and for the past year has been connected with the Board of Public Instruction in the Department of Home Economics and Education for Exceptional Children.

Mr. Cahill was born in Jacksonville and attended local schools before moving to Detroit where he was graduated from high school. During the war, he served four years in the Navy. On June 9 he received his B.S. Degree in Civil Engineering from the Georgia School of Technology in Atlanta. He is a member of the American Society of Civil Engineers.

Mr. and Mrs. Cahill expect to reside in Savannah, Georgia where Mr. Cahill will do further study in his line of work.

Out-of-town guests included Mrs. J.C. Grant, Mr. and Mrs. Don Nutting, Mr. and Mrs. Robert McFarland, all of Tampa, Mrs. Olga Stevens and Mrs. Clarence Hall Smith, god-mother of the bride, both of Miami, and F. H. Sayles, brother of the bride who is attending M.I.T. in Boston, Mass.

On their wedding night George and Mary Lou stayed at Hotel Roosevelt in Jacksonville and, after a light dinner in the hotel's restaurant, retired for the evening.

The next morning, driving a beautiful Lincoln automobile (with air conditioning!) that Aunt Helen had purchased six months earlier and loaned to them for their trip, they drove up the Atlantic coast, stopping along the way in Washington, DC, New York, and then on to visit her brother Jean who was living near Boston. They stayed at the then-popular Howard Johnson's motor hotels all the way up.

During the week after graduating Georgia Tech, George had been staying with his stepmother Flo while preparing for his wedding. A young woman from the Atlanta area named Caroline Weaver had developed more than a passing fancy for George in his last year of school. She had danced with him a few times in previous months at several of the church dances, putting herself in front of him more than any of the other girls, which she perhaps felt entitled her to a claim of sorts. Later when she heard George was getting married, she hunted down his stepmother's address and wrote him a toxic "Dear John" letter, which arrived after George and Mary Lou left for their two-week honeymoon. Flo found the letter in her mail box, "thought it might be important", and opened it. Seeing the contents, she resealed the envelope and, upon his return, gave it to George with her apologies. George immediately showed the letter to Mary Lou who read it, laughed at the woman's gall, and remarked, "I would never write a letter like that."

Once back in Jacksonville at the end of the honeymoon, Allied Chemical called and told George to report to their plant in Savannah, GA on July 1st to begin his training. The newlyweds took the train to Savannah and rented an apartment for the duration. Mary Lou was already a pretty good cook, but the first week in Savannah she made a cake that turned out quite lopsided. When George got home that night she was crying. Yes, the cake was kind of a mess but he said, "That's fine", and they ate it anyway. They liked Savannah very much and went to the beach most weekends.

The couple didn't know a soul and ate out a lot. They stayed there about six weeks while George trained with Dick Shimkus. The Savannah plant was a slightly bigger setup than the one-man-operation he would eventually be manning in Jacksonville. This plant employed three or four men. George was beginning to pick up on crucial methodology.

Once or twice the Shimkus' would have the Cahills over for dinner. George and Mary Lou met Dick's wife and their very young son, also named Dick. Mrs. Shimkus would talk nonstop about all the things her husband and son would do, referring to them constantly as Big Dick and Little Dick. Mary Lou found this highly amusing as the woman went on and on, endlessly recounting how "Big Dick and Little Dick did this…" and "Big Dick and Little Dick did that…" and it was all Mary Lou could do to keep from laughing out loud. The experience served as a cautionary tale to be careful what you name your children.

Then it was back down to the Atlanta plant for more advanced training where Allied manufactured three or four chemical products, including Aluminum Sulfate. This was a much bigger plant than the Savannah installation with about 40-to-50 employees. Training there went on for about another month. Since an employee from the plant had to pass their apartment on his way to work each day, he offered to give George a ride, though he was quite prejudiced against Catholics, always making nasty cracks about them. One day, during their morning ride, after letting go another crude remark, George casually remarked, "You know, I'm Catholic."

The fellow promptly clammed up.

Both George and Mary Lou liked Atlanta a lot. It was a big modern city with lots of culture, restaurants, and things to do. They went to free concerts at a huge theatre every Sunday.

Early on, in discussing aspects of his job, Mary Lou had become well aware of the potential danger in working with sulfuric acid, an integral part of what George would be involved with every day. He assured her every safety precaution was being taken. One night he came home quite late from training and, having forgotten to call, found Mary Lou in tears. She was convinced she'd lost him to a sulfuric acid accident. So distraught was she by the horror of such a possibility, he would never again forget to call.

One evening at dinner George and Mary Lou got on line at a cafeteria where Mary Lou loaded a lot of food on her tray and then, at the table, she suddenly couldn't eat it. After doing this three or four times, she finally realized she'd missed her period and must be pregnant. After much discussion they thought it best to confer with a doctor only after they returned to Jacksonville.

The third and final plant for training was on the outskirts of Macon, GA quite a ways out in the country. The installation was practically an exact duplicate of the one-man Jacksonville plant that George was about to take over, and with an identical operation. Here he trained for about a month.

They got to know the couple at the Macon plant very well and, instead of allowing Mary Lou and George to rent an apartment, as they'd done in Savannah and Atlanta, the couple insisted the newlyweds stay with them in the company bungalow adjacent to the plant. They were lonesome people who didn't really know anyone and were grateful for the company. Mary Lou too was happy for the companionship since, over the past couple of months, she'd mostly been on her own while George was training. And, as this couple had a new baby, Lou was feeling a special kinship.

One evening after dinner the man was lying on his living room couch playing with their newborn, gently jostling it over his head, when the infant emptied the contents of its stomach into his face. A pregnant Mary Lou screamed with laughter. They all did. And one more lesson of motherhood was tucked away for future reference — never hold a freshly fed baby over your head. Good tip.

One weekend these new parents asked if George and Mary Lou would like to see some home movies and, intrigued, they wondered, "Do people do that now?" The man set up a little 8 millimeter projector and started running the most stunning color movies of themselves with their brand new child, remarking that they would be able to revisit these beautiful memories for many years to come. Right away Mary Lou and George recognized the tremendous value of home movies and vowed to get a camera of their own. They later purchased a hand-wound 8mm Keystone movie camera on a payment plan from Sears. The Kodachrome images they shot over the next 50 years would create an enduring record of the Cahill family's remarkable journey.

Altogether, the training tour of the three Georgia plants lasted just over three months. Then it was back home to Jacksonville where George would begin running an installation all his own.

7

Picketville

Allied Chemical had built its newest plant for the manufacture of aluminum sulfate in a little suburb called Picketville, about five miles from downtown Jacksonville, out Route 1 and about a mile off the main road — at 2200 Picketville Road, parallel to I-95 today. Another fellow had been hired several months prior to run the initial operation but the company was quite unhappy, both with his practices and his output, so George was being brought in to replace him. After finishing his training tour of the three Georgia plants, the newlyweds arrived at the Picketville facility in late September of 1948.

The company had built a little house on the property about a hundred yards from the plant where the Cahills could live for a rent of $50.00 a month. There was no furniture to speak of at the beginning; a bed, a small table in the kitchen and couple of chairs. The first year they acquired a couch and a few more household necessities here and there. No thought had been given to air conditioning so the heat simply had to be tolerated. There was never any need for an alarm clock. With the railroad's double-track main line just yards away, every morning at five o'clock a train whistle blasted everyone out of bed. Water was supplied by a well on the property and, as the same big motor-driven pump that fed the plant also fed the house, water for bathing, cooking and cleaning carried with it the pungent aroma of sulfur, which took some getting used to.

There was a shabby little village with a number of questionable characters in residence on the other side of the railroad tracks quite close to where they lived. One day, about a week before their first Christmas in Picketville, the Cahills drove into Jacksonville and, when they got back, someone had broken in and stolen all their Christmas presents. Since Mary Lou's mom was raising German shepherds at the time, she brought one out to them. His name was Baby.

When they first got Baby, George walked him slowly through the village, showing him off so the locals could see there were now teeth to be reckoned with at the little house across the tracks. He then built a fence in the yard all around the house to contain Baby, who was always an outdoor dog and ever alert to strangers. The house had a post box 30 feet beyond the fence out front and the dog would go crazy whenever mail was delivered. But Baby was a loyal, lovable pet and a great watchdog. Very protective.

Flo Cahill's sister Bobbie was married to a doctor named Buster who was a General Practitioner and, though not an obstetrician, Buster agreed to examine Mary Lou to confirm her pregnancy. He even volunteered to deliver their first child at no charge, which sounded ideal since they had no money. But Mary Lou's first delivery did not go easily. In fact it was extremely difficult and she felt it was clumsily handled, declaring, "Never again. Not like that."

Buster had a penchant for fancy cars and expensive distractions and, though it is not known if he was outside his realm of expertise, the birthing experience with a non-obstetric physician for this first time mother left a distinctly negative impression. Whether he had demonstrated a more competent brand of medicine elsewhere in his practice is unknown. But Buster was not well regarded thereafter. Still, though he had not been the doctor she'd have preferred to deliver her children, Mary Lou was saddened to learn that some years later Buster had taken his own life.

Nonetheless, based on her first difficult encounter with childbirth, Mary Lou vowed that, for any future deliveries, only a certified obstetrician would do — no exceptions. Despite any unpleasantness experienced personally by Mary Lou during the procedure itself, her firstborn was a healthy, happy infant and quite the most beautiful first addition to the Cahill family.

Kathleen Theresa Cahill arrived in the world on Monday March 28th 1949 at St. Vincent's Hospital in Jacksonville. When Mary Lou and George brought her home they didn't know any more than the average couple about babies, but were determined to give her their best. Together they went about discovering the most ideal methods of caring for an infant, practices they would improve upon and refine with each subsequent child.

In a letter to Mary Lou's brother Jean, dated June 23rd 1949, when Kathy was three months old, Mabel described her granddaughter with jubilation:

"Everyone is well and Kathleen is super! She's got Mary Lou's blue eyes and a dimple in her right cheek, but she looks a lot like George, except when she gets mad — and then she looks like me! Wouldn't you know that? Her hair is reddish brown and she's got Lou's sweet disposition. Never crys (sp) and only her grandmother spoils her! But she is, without a doubt, the sweetest and strongest baby I've ever seen for her age. They all say I'm 'prejudiced' but I'm not — it's a fact."

The Picketville plant was designed to create one product, aluminum sulfate, which requires two main components for its manufacture. The first being sulfuric acid, one of the most highly corrosive acids known to man. The second is bauxite, a yellowish powder with a high alumina content.

When the railroad delivered a tank car of sulfuric acid, George would fire up a big compressor, putting air into the tank car to offload the acid into a storage tank. In addition, when a hopper car loaded with powdered bauxite would arrive, George got on top of the car and used a long half-inch pipe with air running through it to guide the bauxite to a hatch at the bottom of the car and through an open sliding gate to a screw conveyer below, which then carried the material to an elevator and up into a storage silo.

Since lead is impervious to the highly corrosive properties of sulfuric acid, the plant's storage tank, mixing tank and agitator were lined with lead. In addition, all pipelines and nozzles were made of solid lead. Every now and then one of these elements would develop a sulfuric acid leak and George had learned to use a torch to melt fresh lead onto any cracks or openings to seal the leaks. The process was called "lead burning". Working with these corrosives all day every day, George's work clothes were all full of acid holes, but he never once burned himself or got acid directly on his skin. There are home movies of George in his back yard practicing his golf swing wearing a shirt and pants riddled with acid holes.

One time the company sent a Vice President to inspect the facility who had driven his very expensive Cadillac down with the intent of returning home by plane. He told George, "I'm gonna park this Cadillac in your garage for a while."

The garage was the only secure place to leave the car on the property—which also placed it in very close proximity to the plant's daily chemical operation, making it possible, if not likely, that a loose wrench could fall onto the expensive vehicle, or a spray of acid could accidentally splash onto its finish. When a fellow showed up a week later to take the car off his hands for the V.P., George breathed a sigh of relief. In all other respects, the operation was smooth sailing and the company was consistently happy with George's productivity.

Running the operation on his own, he became proficient at unloading raw material and mixing it in a big mix tank with an agitator. The combination of the sulfuric acid and bauxite would heat up to about 300 degrees. Once it cooled off, the thick mud would separate and the liquid was ready to be pumped into a holding tank. George considered himself quite fortunate having been made to do everything at the start. The experience provided him with valuable knowledge of every detail of the process and his dedication did not go unnoticed.

All the way out in Picketville it wouldn't do to be without transportation and George was acquainted with a car salesman who'd been a good friend of his father's. For a modest price the fellow offered them a huge Plymouth. It was about 7 or 8 years old, a four door in really good condition. It wasn't the most attractive thing, sporting a good deal of rust, so George set up a compressor in the garage at the plant and painted the car black. A year later the same salesman called up and offered George a deal on a better model, a former police car. So he and Mary Lou upgraded their rusty black Plymouth for a gray Dodge in much better overall condition. That car lasted about another couple of years until George finally bought a brand new Ford. Of course these vehicles were all basic transportation, none of which were air conditioned. But they suited the little family well.

In premarital discussions Mary Lou and George initially agreed that perhaps three-to-five children would round out their family nicely. Since medical forms of birth control were not condoned by the church, the couple resorted to an approach known as the "Rhythm Method", a practice touted as popular with Catholics at the time. The method relied upon the woman keeping track of her menstrual cycles, thereby 'predicting' the few days each month she was likely to be fertile. During these intervals the couple would avoid amorous activities. Clinically speaking, it was (and is) the least reliable form of birth control.

"Almost every one of our children was a surprise," George would later recall. "The Rhythm Method meant — hey, you're gonna have a baby."

On Sunday October 15th 1950 George Newton Cahill the Third was born, also at St. Vincent's Hospital, the product of a perfectly normal delivery, and this time at the hands of an experienced obstetrician. The Cahills were now four. With this birth, and with her next, Mary Lou would only have a hospital stay of a couple of days before being sent home without any medical support or follow up.

Whenever she was in the hospital giving birth, and shortly after, George would always take vacation time to stay home and tend to the other children. During one such interval, he invented hot dogs cut up in bean-with-bacon soup as a quick and easy solution for dinner.

George's mother lived five hours away in St. Petersburg with Jack Grant, and running their motel meant they rarely had time to visit, so helping out with the kids wasn't an option for them. Mabel and Helen were somewhat closer in nearby Jacksonville, yet were consumed with scratching out a living for themselves. So, when George was working, Mary Lou was mostly on her own. But she and Kathy were connecting in the way that only a mother and daughter can, with Lou doting on her little girl, giving her all the attention she herself never enjoyed as a youngster.

The Cahill's second child was the son George Jr. had wanted, a little boy to play with, just as his own father had played with him. George III was creatively independent from the first and loved to investigate how things worked, always wandering off on explorations. One day he was missing and George and Mary Lou looked everywhere. With busy railroad tracks nearby, they imagined the worst. They finally discovered the youngster had walked down to the plant by himself, poking around the facility by the acid tank. He got seriously chewed out for that. Another time when little George had disappeared, they looked everywhere and even called the police. Mary Lou finally heard a hiccup and there he had been all along — hiding behind the piano, an older musical instrument that had been donated by a friend who no longer wanted it.

Some time in the early 1950's Jack Grant, the dear man who took on Mae's family in Detroit and saw them through the toughest part of the Great Depression, passed away. George's mother was again on her own. A year or two later Mae met, was courted by, and married Joe Hale, an energetic fellow in his 60's. Together they continued to operate the motel on Hillsborough Avenue in St. Petersburg, but now re-named it the MA-JO Motel.

Though Mary Lou's mom and Aunt Helen were relatively nearby in Jacksonville, they almost never came out to visit. Occasionally the Cahills made the 250 mile drive south to St. Petersburg to visit Don and Mary Nutting, and Mae and Jack Grant. A couple of times they took a trip up to the Boston area to visit Mary Lou's brother Jean Sayles and his family. But finances were always tight and, with no funds to spare, most of their time was spent in and around Picketville.

They kept in close touch with many of Mary Lou's good friends from school and a few of George's from the navy, many of whom also had no money. They'd all pool their resources and get together for picnics, parties and card games at the Picketville house. There was a BBQ pit in the back yard so it was a popular destination for friends who came to visit with their kids. The Cahills frequently went to the beach and, coming back home, the kids were always dog tired. Drive-In movies were also popular and affordable. There was always a swing set with a slide, and sometimes even teeter-totters, under the big outdoor movie screen so parents could keep an eye on their children during the films. The kids would play on the playground and later fall asleep in the car while everyone watched the movies.

Lou's Aunt Helen suggested George might enjoy golf and encouraged him to take it up. She had an almost new set of golf clubs she'd received as a gift that she'd never used and offered them to him. Of course, they were women's clubs so they were somewhat shorter than he was comfortable with. But they were good enough to allow

George to develop some skill. He quickly discovered he enjoyed the game and found time to play whenever he could.

A dear friend of Mary Lou's from school was married to a fellow named Johnny Wilyong. They'd gone over to the Wilyong's house to play cards and Johnny asked, "You wanna see our TV?"

He had the first television set that George ever laid eyes on. It had a huge six-inch screen and it was truly amazing to see.

Johnny owned a nice men's apparel store in Jacksonville and had trouble keeping good help. He needed a part time salesman mostly on Saturday's, their busiest day. He asked if George would be interested in making some extra money. Johnny said he'd train him and, being very poor at the time, George agreed. He went in the next Saturday and trained for the day. The next week he started working regular Saturdays and on odd afternoons for the next year or so. Johnny sold George all his clothes at a discount.

George recalled that Johnny was a nice man, a very handsome guy with a beautiful wife.

On one occasion a large truck showed up to deliver a kitchen appliance and when Mary Lou came to inform George, she found him shaving. He told her to just have the fellow back up as close to the house as he could but to be careful of the septic tank in the yard, the top of which might be difficult for the driver to see.

Preoccupied with waving the trucker into position, Mary Lou lost track of the tank and both she and the driver were amazed when the front of the truck jumped up and the rear dropped through the unnoticed hatch with the back half of truck dipping well into the septic tank. The driver became furious and couldn't manage to get enough traction to pull the truck out.

Ever the engineer, George remembered a friend just across the tracks had a huge jack that he used for the railroad. He borrowed it to hike up the truck's back end, which worked. Unluckily, the moment the truck rolled free, the jack toppled over, fell into the septic tank and disappeared into the putrid muck. Poor Mary Lou could only hang her head, helpless as George's frustration simmered.

George fetched some heavy wire from the plant and, with a bit of noodling around, eventually fashioned a long hook out of it. After half an hour of casting around in the reeking sludge, he managed to fish the heavy tool out of the septic tank. He then dragged the wretched thing down to plant, hooked a hose into the boiler there and used it to steam clean the jack. Of course he never told his neighbor the truth of what happened, except to say his habit was to return a loaned item in as good or better shape than when it was borrowed. The jack was not only cleaner than when he'd picked it up, but very much more so than it had been an hour earlier.

Once back home, the yard, his clothes and the area around the plant boiler all had to be hosed down. And then there was the problem of replacing the septic tank door. The incident served as a valuable lesson in anticipation — learning to look ahead at *every* possible consequence for even the simplest situation. From that day on, and for the rest of their lives, George and Mary Lou gave great consideration to every conceivable outcome for even the smallest decision they ever faced. The practice would serve them well.

The kids would visit the plant, but never during working hours. George III in particular was fascinated by the processes and the manufacturing environment.

George Jr. was salaried and could schedule his own hours, so long as all the work got done. He'd start early and quit when finished, sometimes by early afternoon. He met all his production quotas, turning out finished mixes of the expected volume of chemicals each day. There were pumps used to manufacture the product, and also to pump the finished products into a truck or tank car.

In his first five years with Allied Chemical, George did everything from cleaning toilets, receiving raw materials and maintaining machinery, to packing and shipping, as well as record keeping, invoicing, and billing — all of which left him with a well rounded overall perspective of a chemical plant's operations top to bottom. It also taught him that the most effective manager was one who knew, in detail, how to do every job in a plant. Years later, when he finally achieved a management position, he would make a regular practice of keeping his hand in at every level while staying up on the latest manufacturing and transport methods and developments.

George was included in all of Allied's supervisory memos distributed to managers at plants throughout the country. As the manager of the company's one-man shop in Picketville, he was regularly kept up on, not only how managers communicated with each other throughout North American operations, but on every technical, personnel and protocol issue being discussed, wrestled with, and solved at every level. He paid especially close attention to corporate communiqués, which, in essence, provided a master class in management do's and don'ts, and effectively built a knowledge base that would pay off handsomely down the road.

John Sundy, the VP who had originally hired him, corresponded regularly and visited the plant once or twice a week. George kept gently reminding John that he wanted to progress and get away from being a one-man operation. He needed to grow in the company.

Baby had been a good dog for the five years the Cahills spent in Picketville, greeting family and friends, warding off trespassers and loving the children. She died in the summer of their last year in Florida. As a family they said their goodbyes to Baby and, shortly thereafter, said hello to the newest Cahill.

On Friday, July 10th 1953, Mary Lou gave birth, again at St. Vincent's Hospital, to her third child Susan Ann Cahill, a second daughter and a bright, smiling addition to the family.

Right on the heels of Susan's arrival, and without warning, a call came for George from Allied's corporate headquarters: "There's a job opening in Ohio and you were recommended for it by John Sundy."

8

Cleveland

Late in the summer of 1953, in advance of the family's move north, George flew up to Ohio to look for a place to live. After unsuccessfully scouring the housing market for a week, one of the foremen at the Allied plant finally mentioned he owned a house on West 100th Street that he'd be happy to lease. It was perfect.

Since the company was paying for the move, Mary Lou and the kids were to fly up to Cleveland. Having never been on a plane before, the trip was something of an ordeal for her, with a four-year-old, a three-year-old, and a newborn. Waiting at the gate to meet his family at the airport in Cleveland, a fellow came off the plane, eyeballed George and asked, "Are you *Daddy*?"

"I think so."

The fellow jerked a thumb back toward the plane. "Your wife is having some trouble."

Mary Lou had gotten sick on the plane. The journey for the most part had been fine but the plane made a stop along the way and the last leg of the flight had been rough for her. Despite this rocky first experience, in years to come, Mary Lou would evolve into a seasoned air traveler.

The house at 3280 West 100th Street would need some work. George eventually purchased the house and, in the seven years they lived there, he painted it twice, both times perched atop a rickety 40-foot ladder to reach the tip of the roof line, a feat he recalled with pride.

Mary Lou's very first priority in this new city was finding a church. The family attended every Sunday. The local school was one long block away and just across a busy boulevard, so it would be a short walk for the kids. Right away she busied herself organizing the household.

Cleveland was a major industrial center as well as being a St. Lawrence Seaway port, right at the mouth of the Cuyahoga River. Perched on the southern shore of Lake Erie, and with Canada skirting the far north shore, the wind and chill of winter easily got into one's bones. The coolest months were January and February with an average high of 34°F and average low of 22°F. Aside from George, who'd grown up in Detroit, this level of cold was new to the rest of the family. It was also their first experience with snow. The national average snowfall was 28 inches, but Cleveland saw almost double that at 54 inches every year. Mary Lou had to get used to driving in snow, which fell frequently and in big storms.

Ohio summers didn't have anything close to the heat of Florida summers but, being so close to the river and the lake, the dense humidity made for a muggy season from May through September. And there was another phenomenon new to them — tornadoes. A tornado warning meant everyone rushed to the basement and huddled in a corner for protection until the danger had passed. Infrequent though they were, tornadoes threatened mostly in May, June and July. After one tornado struck, the family decided to tour the nearby damaged area. George remembered marveling a the sight of an 8-foot two-by-four that had been punched like an arrow directly through the trunk of a full grown tree. The physics of it simply staggered him.

Just three houses away on West 100th Street lived the Fialcos. Mr. Fialco was active with the Boy Scouts and was very well liked in the community. His teenage daughter Lois was beloved by all. According to Mary Lou and George, she was "the very best babysitter in the world." The kids absolutely adored Lois. And she just loved the Cahills.

She was always there, even when she wasn't babysitting, just to spend time with the children. She was practically part of the family.

Unlike the Picketville plant's one-man operation, which had only manufactured liquid aluminum sulfate, the Cleveland facility manufactured it in both liquid and solid form, and on a much larger scale, in addition to producing sulfuric acid in bulk.

George started out as foreman of Allied's General Chemical Division in charge of the aluminum sulfate operation supervising about 15-to-20 people. Along the way he also learned the sulfuric acid manufacturing process and became proficient in leading that team as well. Solid and liquid products left the plant by box car, tank car and truck. Sulfuric acid could be dangerous stuff, but the plant had all the best protective features to make it safe to work with. Aside from being the most corrosive of acids, it was an incredibly common industrial component used in a wide variety of processes, including waterworks, steel manufacturing and, of course, making aluminum sulfate. To meet market demands the company's output had to be prodigious.

Mary Lou was thrilled with the amount of culture that Cleveland had to offer compared to Picketville and Jacksonville. A few years earlier in 1950 the Cleveland Browns had joined the National Football League and managed to win the national championship in their first year, a feat they repeated again in 1954 and 55. Cleveland had a symphony orchestra, and amazing art and science museums. Mary Lou was finally in her element, a big city with plenty of parks, restaurants, theaters and shopping venues, plus a wonderful mass transit system that made getting around incredibly convenient.

There were also golf courses.

About eight or ten men at work would team up every Friday around four o'clock and head out together to play a round of golf. George was invited along and soon became a regular. Nobody had ever taken lessons. They'd all just learned on their own. Continuing to struggle along with the set of women's clubs George had inherited from Mary Lou's Aunt Helen was no longer an option. That very next Christmas Mary Lou gave George his first serious set of golf clubs — men's clubs. At the end of the season the Allied team had always held its own tournament and that next year George took home the title cup.

Mary Lou was as good as her word, fulfilling the promise she made to George's father that he'd always have time to go out with his friends. More importantly, though, she and George made certain to reserve time for themselves as well. Coordinating with his work schedule and counter-scheduling her own household agenda, she carefully set aside time for the two of them to go out to dinner, a show, or to the many parties hosted by plant employees. For the most part, careers and parenthood dominated Mary Lou and George's thinking. But remembering how to be a couple was forever their highest priority. Lois Fialco was always happy, if not anxious, to stay with the children, bless her heart. And so, out the Cahills went.

Sometime in the early 1950's Mabel married again. This time, and briefly, to Clyde Gardner who, at the time, was the orchestra leader at the Hotel Roosevelt in Jacksonville. In Cahill home movies, a brief glimpse of Mr. Gardner appears. It's unclear how long the union lasted, though it's not thought to be for much more than a year, if that much.

Once again on her own, Mary Lou's mother migrated north to live with the Cahills in Cleveland for a couple of years between 1955 and '58. Mabel was multi-talented. She could do everything. She adored her grandchildren and, especially on holidays, drafted the kids into her decorating schemes, stenciling the windows with snowflakes and angels. Also a capable ceramic artist, she molded, painted and fired plates, bowls and decorative items as gifts. Her granddaughter Susan still has a plate Mabel made and signed, "Christmas 1952". A particular family favorite of hers was a handmade Santa Claus statue that graced the Cahill home every Christmas for years to come, signed on the bottom with her last married name, "Gardner".

Living with the Cahills presented challenges nonetheless. All her life Mary Lou had battles back and forth with her mother, who had the same contentious relationship with her sister Helen. Both Mary Lou and George begrudgingly conceded Mabel was a hard person to live with. While living with the Cahills, she had no real income so George scraped together a small monthly allowance so Mabel could have a bit of spending money. When she eventually qualified for government assistance and started receiving regular and substantial checks from the state, Mabel couldn't understand why George stopped her allowance and became quite angry with him.

"I never heard a woman curse like she did", George recalled.

She traveled in an old station wagon with her german shepherds as companions and kept a loaded rifle in her room. For some reason, one midnight Mabel Rominger had gotten upset yet again and, without asking George to move his car, drove off across the lawn and went back to Jacksonville.

As a youngster getting no real answers about her father from Mabel or Aunt Helen, Mary Lou never stopped wondering about Charlie Kramer. Was he alive? And if so, where? Having always relied on the church to guide her, in 1955 she inquired about the possibility of locating Charles Kramer through the national network of churches. The local diocese made inquiries and, through a church in California, they located Mary Lou's father. She finally made contact and Charlie agreed to cross the country to meet his daughter and her family.

Cahill home movies recorded some of the visit, which included Charlie, his wife Jane, along with his sister and her husband. George recalled the visit was pleasant enough and Mary Lou finally got to see her real father face to face for the first time, capturing in the exchange some small sense of his personality and general good humor. The Kramers and their companions were earnest drinkers of beer and kept pushing Mary Lou to join them, though, having never cared for beer, she repeatedly declined. By all appearances Mary Lou was pleased with the encounter and Charlie too seemed to enjoy the visit and getting to know his daughter a bit. They promised to keep in touch and the Kramer party returned to California.

Charlie and Jane traveled back to visit Mary Lou's family a second time in the Spring of 1957. George's mother had lost her husband Joe Hale a year or so earlier and, in the summer of '57, Mae journeyed up from Florida with her new husband Bob Happ to spend time with the family. Cahill home movies show both these family visits as being jovial occasions.

At work, George's diligence was rewarded with a number of promotions and subsequent pay increases. Ironically, with each professional success came a boost at home. George recalled, "It seemed like every time I got a raise, we'd have another baby."

With her first three children, Mary Lou had been ushered out of the hospital within two or three days of the births, feeling completely unprepared to tend to herself or the children at home. In Cleveland she'd made a friend whose husband was head of Obstetrics at a local hospital. The man was "a wonderful doctor" who absolutely insisted that, after the birth, the mother would stay at least ten days in the hospital for a complete recovery before taking the newborn home. Mary Lou just loved that. During their years in Cleveland, she and George managed to produce four more children, all of them born at Fairfield Hospital:

- Michael Joseph Cahill - Born Saturday January 29, 1955
- Christopher Douglas Cahill - Born Tuesday February 14, 1956
- Mary Melissa Cahill - Born Sunday September 21, 1958

• Deborah Elizabeth Cahill - Born Tuesday July 26, 1960

With the always pleasant and ever-accommodating Lois Fialco lending a hand with the kids, Mary Lou's life at home was made significantly less hectic. As the family grew, the Cahill's traded in the 4-door Ford for their first station wagon.

At Allied Chemical, George continued to assert himself with management, graduating through the ranks to assistant manager for the entire plant. However, his next promotion would take him out of the country. In September 1960, about six weeks after Deborah was born, the Cahills were bound for Canada. There were many sad goodbyes to be made but by far the most heartbreaking was that of dear, sweet Lois Fialco who cried the hardest while bidding farewell to the children she'd come to love for seven years.

Mary Lou and George kept in touch with the Fialcos for some time after and were happy to learn that eventually Lois married and became a mother with a family of her own. Even up through the 1980's, Mary Lou had continued to exchange Christmas cards with Lois.

9

Vancouver

Since Allied Chemical was again paying for George's latest transfer, the Cleveland house was sold and packed up, a moving company engaged, and everyone piled into the family station wagon. Motel and restaurant bills along the way were picked up by the company. Mary Lou was now well practiced at traveling with so many youngsters and started this cross country journey armed with a bag of toys and games that she kept hidden under the car's front seat, a habit she would employ on every car trip the family would take from then on. Whenever the children became restless, she'd pull out the bag and produce a new diversion.

Seeing the vastness of the American landscape roll past, Mary Lou never missed an opportunity to point out key features; deserts, forests, mountains, landmarks, and historic sites along the way. It was all part of her ongoing effort to give her children the broadest possible experience. Questions were constantly posed aloud: "Who can tell me how many states we'll be traveling through on our way to Vancouver?" Or, "I'll bet no one can tell me what kind of birds those are." Or even, "Who can spot license plates from the most states?" Sing alongs and word games made for a memorable trip.

Having finally arrived at the northern U.S. border to cross from Washington state into British Columbia, Canada, George was asked by a Customs agent, "What brings you to Canada?"

"I'm taking a new job."

"What's the job?"

"I'm replacing the supervisor of the Allied Chemical plant in Vancouver."

"Oh — you're replacing the Great Stone Face!"

Amazingly the Canadian customs agents actually knew the man from whom George would be taking over, a fellow mysteriously known as "The Great Stone Face". The nickname was confirmed by employees at the plant, though its origin would never be explained. Interestingly, the Great Stone Face, a father of twelve children, was being replaced by a father of seven.

30 miles north of the U.S. border was Vancouver. It was September 1960 and it rained every day during their first month in Canada. The region was dense with greenery and outrageously beautiful. British Columbia was lumber country. Fog was intense and frequent, often impenetrable.

An exploratory visit prior to the family's move had permitted George to locate a house under construction in the suburb of Coquitlam, elevated above Vancouver City about eight miles east of the metropolis. By the time they arrived, the house was just being finished. Handsomely situated on a spacious corner lot, it occupied just over a quarter acre at 1751 Harbour Drive.

After growing up in Detroit, and most recently spending years in Ohio, Canada may well have seemed an intimidating climate change. However Coquitlam benefitted greatly from being smack dab in the middle of one of the warmest regions in Canada with an average yearly temperature of 50°F degrees. The region experienced minimal snowfall, and any snow that did arrive was usually wet and melted away within a few days. In addition to the mountains that were just offshore on Vancouver Island, which shielded the coastline from the ocean's bitter winds, a warm Japanese current that swept up into the northern Pacific kept the region from getting too cold in the winter. The result was a mostly rainy but relatively moderate climate year round. Summer months rarely peaked above 89°F.

Temperatures in December and January only sporadically dipped down to freezing. So, with an abundance of rain, the only genuine travel concerns involved occasionally icy roads and inordinately dense fog. Coquitlam was situated up the hill from Vancouver City and to the east. On the opposite side of the mountain, just a bit further to the east, more traditional Canadian temperatures prevailed and that area would be blanketed by huge snows.

Compared to Allied's much larger facility in Ohio, the Vancouver plant was a somewhat smaller operation. In his first solo supervisory position, George oversaw the manufacture of two products — aluminum sulfate, something he was already an old hand at producing, and sulfuric acid, a process he'd become proficient at during his years in Cleveland. Allied's Vancouver facility maintained a contingent of 35-to-40 workers and ran an additional warehousing operation that stocked various products, imported from other Allied facilities to be distributed and sold locally.

Being a port city, Vancouver's local manufacturing relied heavily on shipping, both by rail and water. Waterway shipments to and from the Allied plant were subservient to local tides. Railway cars (both tank cars of liquid materials and open-topped hopper cars for solids) were floated in on a barge during high tide. As the tide went down, the inbound flat bottomed barge settled onto a solid, flat construction just under the water, which consequently brought the rails atop of the barge into perfect alignment with a rail line on shore. A pulley system was then employed to roll the rail car off the barge and along a railway siding up next to the warehouse for offloading solids, or alongside a tank for offloading liquids. At the next low tide any outgoing rail cars were rolled back onto the barge and, come high tide, the now-floating barge was tug-boated away. The timing of tides varied from day to day, and tide tables published in the daily paper were regularly consulted to schedule all barge activity.

The plant's chemical operations were crucially dependent on a significant amount of water but the process didn't draw on the city's water supply. Instead, with Vancouver's tremendous natural precipitation, rainwater was collected in a concrete reservoir on a hillside just above the plant and was then funneled underground directly to the plant. Some years before, being situated right in the heart of lumber country, a local company had cleverly conceived a method for making a reliable underground pipeline out of wood. George got to observe such a pipeline employed for this rainwater transfer operation and was duly impressed as he had only ever seen metal pipe so employed.

Under his supervision, the plant's operations ran smoothly during regular daylight hours, with little if any call for overtime, a pleasant enough change from his unwieldy Cleveland schedule.

One of the most striking aspects of life in Vancouver overall was the predominance of fog. It was the heaviest George and Mary Lou had ever seen, before or since. Allied's facility was quite close to the Pacific shipping lanes, and fog horns from passing ships could be incredibly loud. Fog regularly came and went throughout the year but was most prevalent in the Fall. It was so dense that many times while traveling to work he would easily miss the plant entrance from the main road, cruising right past it just feet away. Instead of snow days, the entire community experienced fog days. The dense, billowy soup would roll in, last for almost a week at a time, and cause most outdoor activities to shut down, including driving. Rain was also frequent, steady and relentless. An optimistic sort could eventually become accustomed to it since it produced such beautiful countryside with lush forests, abundant greenery and a prodigious variety of flowers. But it demanded an entirely new mindset to which the Cahills were unused.

Coquitlam locals were the most affable sort of people. Fishing was considerably more than a pastime and a neighbor who was an avid fisherman would always return from his trips with a bounty for his neighbors, including an enormous piece of fresh salmon for Mary Lou, which she always loved.

The Brice family, the loveliest of next door neighbors, had for many years operated a thriving family concern but the unions had driven them out of business and they were forced to close up shop and retire. On one weekend Mr. Brice observed George struggling to cut his grass with a rotary blade push-mower and offered him the regular use of their power mower to cut his big yard. George Jr. and George III took turns running the huge self-propelled contraption all over the property.

Mary Lou made friends easily and a number of families in the neighborhood warmed up to her right away. As a woman with a powerful sense of color and proportion, she was anxious to fill out the broad landscape of her new yard, a fresh canvas begging to be painted in bold strokes. There was a very nice older Russian gentleman working at the plant with George who had an English wife and the woman was a great, enthusiastic gardener. One spring day Mary Lou went to visit her for a bit of advice and came back with the family station wagon packed to overflowing with plants, seedlings and bulbs that the English woman had thrust upon her.

"Just drop any seed or bulb into this Vancouver soil and stand back. They grow so fast they'll practically jump out of the ground."

With the helping hands of her children, Mary Lou installed all kinds of flowers and plants around the yard and, as promised, they practically burst right out, dozens and dozens of the most beautiful blossoms and ferns.

Mary Lou was a loyal devotee of publications like Reader's Digest, Ladies Home Journal and Better Homes and Gardens. She constantly clipped recipes, gardening and decorating tips from their pages. One such tip recommended that roses thrive on iron oxide and calcium so she buried old tin cans and egg shells at the base of her rose bushes and boy, did they bloom. Bulb flowers like daffodils, crocuses, irises, tulips and hyacinths peppered the front and back yards. Vancouver springs and summers produced a kaleidoscope of glorious blossoms. In Mary Lou, the Englishwoman had found a talented protégé indeed.

A number of large rocks and enormous car-sized boulders were also natural to the area. A particularly massive hunk of granite half the size of a house formed the centerpiece of a grassy island in a culdesac a few blocks away on Shasta Court. It was a favorite climbing place simply dubbed "Big Rock" by the neighborhood kids. Another gigantic subterranean boulder ran beneath the Cahill home, a portion of which surfaced in the middle of the back yard. It was too prominent to be concealed so Mary Lou and George made it the centerpiece of the patio and planted flowers around it. A tall cedar fence enclosed the back yard and, with a few large leftover planks, George constructed a huge sandbox in the yard's back corner up against the fence.

He also recognized opportunity in a great discarded pile of sulfur-yellow brick at the Allied plant. The brick had been specially fired with a glassy finish to resist the corrosion of sulfuric acid. He loaded up the station wagon with several small shipments of the abandoned masonry, building up a collection at home. He finally ordered a giant truckload of sand, which was dumped on the street just outside the back yard gate. Before he could put his boys to work shoveling the sand and wheelbarrowing it into the yard, children from the neighborhood had already commandeered the pile, racing up and down it, building forts and playing in it with toy trucks. The sand was used to set the bricks for the new backyard patio, a weekend project with the boys, and the leftover supply filled up the new sandbox. Suddenly the Cahill's back yard became the most popular destination for neighborhood kids.

The Coquitlam house wasn't huge but it was roomy enough, a split-level arrangement with the upper floor being flush with the street out front and the lower level opening out onto a nice little back yard. The house was topped with cedar shake shingles that held up well in the rainy weather.

Creativity was called upon to accommodate a bustling family of nine. Mary Lou and George had the master bedroom, while the four girls shared the remaining two bedrooms upstairs. George built out the basement. In addition to a modest family room, he added a half bath, a smallish bedroom with bunk beds for the two younger boys, and a slightly larger bedroom for George III, which incidentally had its own separate door that opened to the back yard patio.

The living room featured an eight foot wide picture window, allowing one to easily look down into the back yard while affording a spectacular view over the roofs of the houses sloping down the hill behind and on into the city of Vancouver some miles below — that is, when the view was unobstructed by weather. There was also a wood burning fireplace, which was easily supplied by picking through the nearby forest for fallen timber and kindling.

Having achieved her lifelong ambition to be a full time mother and wife, Mary Lou excelled at organizing and maintaining a busy household. She was an exceptional and resourceful cook, orchestrating big breakfasts, sending kids off to with good lunches and managing unique and wholesome dinners for a small army. Keeping up with grocery shopping, laundry, ironing and mending, house cleaning and decorating, plus doctors and dentists — and all while pregnant during her first year in Canada — made for an exhausting and never ending schedule. Yet this energetic mother of seven, designed as she was, proved equal to the task.

Mary Lou gave birth to her eighth and final child, Lisa Diane Cahill, on Thursday August 9th 1962 at Vancouver General Hospital, the only one of her children not born on American soil. Shortly after the birth, while still in the hospital, it was discovered Mary Lou's reproductive system had developed significant enough complications that she would not be able to sustain another pregnancy. The difficult decision was made, then and there, to tie off her fallopian tubes.

Knowing she had contributed to more than her share of the population, Mary Lou traded whatever grief she felt for some small degree of relief that her childbearing years were now behind her.

Some years later, during a conversation with Mary Lou, a very young Lisa asked, "Mom, are you ever going to have another baby?"

Mary Lou chuckled. "That would be one rich baby. Because we'd be suing the doctor in Vancouver who was supposed to have tied my tubes."

Then with a laugh she added, "Talk about closing the barn door after the horses have escaped!"

Not long after Lisa was born, Mary Lou invited her father to Coquitlam. Charlie and Jane put in an appearance, met their latest grandchild, and seemed to generally enjoy the Vancouver sites.

Social creatures that they were, fellow employees at the Vancouver plant held a lot of parties. These good folks maintained a tradition of celebration that closely resembled making oneself at home. At one such affair, George recalled a visiting salesman, where the fellow just happily sat working a jigsaw puzzle the entire time. Nothing more was required of a guest. These get togethers were anything but boisterous and everyone felt familiar enough to relax and simply enjoy.

Mary Lou and George went out to eat quite a bit, as restaurants in the area were numerous and varied, many specializing in a particular favorite of theirs — seafood.

Family day trips sometimes dipped south into the states to where rivers met lakes and everyone could marvel as big ships moved gracefully through the massive locks. Another favorite family outing would take them to a nearby favorite, Stanley Park, with its jaw-droppingly tall trees and lush landscapes. Vancouver was a city that excelled at showing off.

On July 10, 1962, Everett Perry Rominger passed away on his farm from an acute cerebral hemorrhage related to cardio vascular disease. Mabel and Helen traveled back to Indiana to attend their father's funeral at Ames Chapel Cemetery. At the interment, they noticed their own mother's nearby grave only sported a small, almost insignificant marker compared to those of other late members of the family. This so infuriated the sisters that, in a spontaneous act of loyalty to their beloved mother, they scraped together enough resources to replace Cena Bostock Rominger's tiny marker with a great polished granite monument that far outsized every other gravestone in the family's section of the cemetery, including, and especially, their father's. The resulting dismay exhibited by the rest of the surviving family was the very reaction Mabel and Helen had hoped to elicit.

Whatever his professional situation, George was always pushing to advance, to move up through the ranks at Allied, to make more money. Without having to resort to self-promotion, it was always evident to management that George brought tremendous value to the company beyond his current discipline.

As part of their close collaboration, Mary Lou and George would discuss at length any possible transfer, investigating every pro and con. How much of a potential salary boost might make a move worthwhile? How might it be favorably balanced against finding new doctors, new dentists, new schools — new everything? Even the smallest considerations were preceded by days, if not months, of discussion. From the very first, the two of them had agreed that George's career would not be his own. It was absolutely an equal partnership with Mary Lou. Every move up the ladder was preceded by plenty of in-depth exploration. It would never be just George making the decision. There were simply too many variables to consider, not the least of which were huge changes at home and often a radical change of climate.

George had been asking Allied for a long time not to stay in one job for too long. Then came word of an installation in Quebec that was making a major changeover from its iron ore operation to the processing of zinc ore. When an offer was put on the table of Assistant Plant Manager at this facility on the other side of Canada, it seemed the answer to a prayer. Plus the money would be a bit more than he'd been seeing in Vancouver.

Yes, making such a big move in the middle of a school year was problematic. But wouldn't the benefits outweigh the inconvenience?

10

Valleyfield

George and Mary Lou were suddenly faced with the prospect of moving across Canada in the middle of winter. With the Valleyfield plant undergoing such a huge transition, they needed someone pronto to supervise the changeover. George was definitely their man, but only a fool would cross the breadth of Canada with eight kids in December. Yet the company was anxious for George to relocate to Quebec at the earliest possibility. Their new client wasn't willing to wait until summer.

Mary Lou was a great cross-continental planner with toys, games, and the occasional camp cookout. The family departed Vancouver three days before Christmas 1962 and would mostly be stopping at restaurants along the way because the company was paying for the move so, why not? For a continental crossing in December, it made sense to drop down into California and then head across the U.S., bypassing the harshest winter weather, and then hop back north, reentering Canada from the east. By this time Charlie and Jane Kramer had retired and were living in Anaheim just south of Los Angeles. Anaheim also happened to be the home of Disneyland, which had opened just 7 years earlier.

"Dad and Jane were happy to put us up for a day or two on our way to Valleyfield," Mary Lou recalled. She would get to see her father one more time over Christmas 1962. The holiday would be meager on the road so, as a Christmas present for the kids, George loaded the six older children into the car and treated them to a day at Disneyland on Christmas Eve, while Mary Lou and the two youngest stayed behind visiting with the Kramers.

Home movies captured by George show some of the children's adventures at the popular amusement park, which would be the highlight of their trip across the states.

Having raced to sell the Coquitlam house and pack up the family, Mary Lou was deeply saddened that it wasn't going to be much of a Christmas morning for the kids. It was all the more touching that, when they awoke Christmas morning, Jane Kramer had two wrapped gifts for each of the Cahill children already nestled under the Christmas tree. Mary Lou recalled being quite moved by Jane's thoughtfulness and generosity. Charlie topped off the moment by doling out a shiny new silver dollar to every child.

Packing the family back in the car the day after Christmas, Mary Lou bid a fond farewell to the Kramers. It's unclear whether Mary Lou saw much of her father after this, if at all. Charlie passed away on June 25th 1975 at the age of 88.

The Cahills landed at their new house in Quebec the day after New Years 1963. At the Valleyfield plant, Allied Chemical had long been burning pyrites ore to excise sulfur, which was then used to make sulfuric acid. The process was this installation's bread and butter, utilizing two enormous furnaces, each one featuring a 30-foot-high cylinder. Sulfur ore was poured onto grates in the cylinders where the sulfur was burned out of it.

The new client's company had its own mine that generated a steady supply of zinc ore and when they approached Allied, the idea was to use the Valleyfield facility to excise zinc from their ore in a somewhat identical fashion as the current sulfur process.

Interestingly, the zinc ore also happened to contain sulfur, which the process would similarly separate as a byproduct. The excised zinc was shipped off to the new client and the sulfur, which the client didn't want, was a valuable byproduct for Allied. The company would still be making money from their traditional process of sulfur production, but with their zinc client providing the ore and paying for all the processing.

George was being brought in as the new assistant plant manager to supervise the changeover from burning pyrites ore to burning zinc ore. One of the plant's two furnaces would continue to manufacture straight sulfur while the second furnace was shut down and converted for the zinc process. Once the newly renovated furnace was up and running, the remaining furnace would also be shut down and converted as well.

The June after arriving in Valleyfield, George was required to go up to Northern Canada to inspect the client's new mine. The zinc company had built an entire village for its mining families, who numbered about 300 people. It was rough terrain getting there with no roads at all. The only way to get back and forth from the village was by rail. The train consisted primarily of several open-topped gondola cars used for ore transport plus a couple of passenger cars.

Making the trip only once a week, the train departed early in the morning, stopping maybe two or three times along the way to pick up a few local Indians and perhaps a canoe or two. This was how locals made their way to remote hunting and fishing territories. The Indians would ride in the passenger car and hop off at a predetermined stop. The train continued up to the mine and, once there, George had with a limited window of time to make his inspection. If he wasn't back on board by 4:00 PM, he'd be stuck there until the train returned the following week.

At the mine, George closely observed and made notes of everything they did. He found it extremely interesting, an entirely self contained operation in this totally isolated little village, built exclusively for the mining of zinc ore. Being so far north, even in summer it was still remarkably cold. Product was transported from northern Canada on the same train that George used to ride there and back. Since the ore was mined wet, it arrived in open gondolas as one solid frozen block. Once in Valleyfield, the train's cars were rolled into a gigantic heated building and left there to thaw out for a day. Then it was off to the furnaces.

After familiarizing himself with the end-to-end process, George supervised shutting down the first of the two ore furnaces and began orchestrating its transition.

Back at home, however, fresh challenges were presenting themselves daily.

Valleyfield, Quebec would test every bit of endurance the Cahills could muster. The spoken language was (and still remains) overwhelmingly French Canadian and, in the early 1960's, English speakers were blatantly scorned. Even with Mary Lou's bubbly personality, her sweet-natured disposition cut no slack with the locals. Cultural venues were rare, if they existed at all. Hockey and ice skating predominated. Not one movie theater was easily reachable. Even the most vaguely decent shopping was over an hour away in Montreal, weather permitting.

Valleyfield, as it is known by English speakers (it's French Canadian name is Salaberry-De-Valleyfield), is an island in the St. Lawrence river and is bordered by Lake St. Francis. Owing to its numerous rivers and canals, Valleyfield had been nicknamed the Venice of Quebec, though no one could convince Mary Lou of any analogous charms.

The climate was a predominantly gray gloom with an average high temperature in the summer of 69°F. December through February averaged between 20°F and 14°F — not including windchill factors. The local lake froze completely solid in winter months and vehicles were easily driven onto it. As part of an annual winter festival, one-meter cubes of ice were cut out to erect a modest castle on the lake and horse-drawn sleigh rides were common. But the iciness of the environment was not limited to the weather.

The Cahills frequently traveled back to the U.S., including an especially big trip once each season to outfit the family. Clothing was much, much cheaper in the states, and local stores, of the few that existed, were incredibly expensive. Of course, once shopping was completed, while returning back across the border from the U.S., Mary Lou made the kids each wear two of three layers of clothes so they wouldn't have to declare the purchases, thereby avoiding a duty tax.

"Oh no, we were just visiting. No shopping. Nothing to claim!"

Immediately after clearing Customs of course, then came the complaints from the back—"We're hot!"

The road approaching the U.S. border from the Canadian side, and then coming back again from the states, involved a series of ribbon-like hills with numerous sudden dips, swoops and curves, always prompting cries of, "Go fast, daddy — go *fast!!*"

With an approving flash of Mary Lou's eyes, George obligingly gunned the engine, setting off a chorus of gleeful squeals.

Valleyfield had two school systems: the French system, which enjoyed the lion's share of local resources, money and quality teachers; and the English system, which was treated as second class, receiving only the dregs, the raggedy leftovers of funding, amenities and personnel. Mary Lou's own Catholic education had been a superbly rich experience. But now, confronted with a segregated and marginalized system, her children were not receiving anything near the educational basics they were due.

The little brick house the Cahills rented at 158 Rue St. Charles was much too small for a family of ten. There ended up being very little money and Mary Lou had no real friends to speak of. The welcome she had known in Cleveland and Vancouver was nowhere to be found here.

To make things worse, some months after George moved to Valleyfield, he learned that a dear Russian gentleman he formerly worked with had met with a terrible accident at the Vancouver plant. While unloading a tank, a hose had broken loose and drenched him in sulfuric acid, killing him, thus lending credence to a long feared nightmare of Mary Lou's. Not long after that, in November of 1963, President John F. Kennedy was assassinated and the world as she knew it seemed to be receding further and further away.

The entire purpose of Mary Lou's life was dedicated to the quality upbringing of her eight wonderful children. Yet their education now was being severely compromised by an unfeeling, inflexible and underfunded school system.

Not one to let circumstance command her children's fate, Mary Lou took an active hand in learning all she could about this alien school district with its operations and protocols securely bound up in a bureaucratic morass.

The physical premises of her children's school was another story altogether. Mary Lou was stunned to learn paper materials, flammable supplies and records were being stored in the basement next to a giant coal-fueled boiler, posing a considerable fire hazard.

Even more staggering was the discovery that the school's two-story fire escape consisted of a dilapidated wooden affair with splintered railings and broken steps. The school's principal had considered it so unsafe that his solution was to simply lock the second floor fire exit door, thereby avoiding any risk of "injury" on the stair — but effectively blocking any safe escape should a fire break out.

Mary Lou was furious. She carefully put together a strongly worded statement, written out in great detail, to present to the school board. Much to his surprise, George was informed he would be giving the presentation.

"But it's your presentation. Why am I giving it?"

"Because the board is all men and they won't listen to a woman."

Of course she was right.

George and Mary Lou attended the next school board meeting and George read Mary Lou's presentation just as she had written it. During the speech all pressing hazards, dire consequences and reasonable solutions were delineated, including a generous assertion that engineers at her husband's plant would happily design a new steel fire escape for the school. As predicted, the board listened to the man and subsequently agreed to the woman's proposal.

George indeed had Allied's engineers draw up and deliver the promised plans, funds were approved, the new fire escape was installed, the fire door unlocked, and the boiler room was cleared of flammable materials.

As a result of Mary Lou's proactive stance, the school's principal was also fired and replaced.

In light of everything confronting them, her victory with the school board felt hollow and short lived. It could not begin to quell the despair welling up in her. Keenly aware that his wife's emotional health was at hazard, George scheduled a three-day getaway weekend with Mary Lou in Washington, D.C. where she could consult with an english-speaking priest.

It's unclear why they chose Washington, but once again, through the Catholic network of churches, the D.C. diocese assigned a member of the clergy to meet with them. The man with whom they met was a young priest but well trained in family counseling. He took his time, listening with great care to every detail of Mary Lou's plight.

After due consideration, his recommendation was firm and concise — "Get your family out of Valleyfield as fast as you can."

With fifteen stellar years under his belt, studded with regular raises and highly recommended promotions, George was in very good stead with Allied Chemical. He knew, if the need arose, he could find a job anywhere. Mary Lou's health and happiness were his primary consideration.

The moment they returned to Valleyfield, George promptly informed Allied that either he would quit or they would find him a position elsewhere. Very much elsewhere.

There was no third option.

Management liked him a lot and quickly agreed to do what they could. Two weeks later they came back to him with an opening for an assistant manager at a plastics plant in Pennsylvania. Every previous transfer had involved a salary boost, but this would have to be more of a lateral move.

"It's available now, or you can wait," they offered, adding the firm assurance that, given just a bit more time, they could certainly find something more attractive.

George and Mary Lou didn't want to wait

"We'll take it."

11

Coal Country

George grabbed the first available flight to a little coal mining community in central southeastern Pennsylvania to check in with his new work place — Allied Chemical's Fabricated Products Division. With a population of about 20,000, the little town of Pottsville covered just over four square miles and had made its bones in 1790 when a hunter named Necho Allen awoke one morning surrounded by flames, or so the legend goes. His campfire had ignited an outcropping of coal on a nearby hillside, the discovery of which set off a coal mining craze in the region.

In Pottsville, George met with his boss, Guy Walters. The position of Assistant Plant Manager seemed agreeable enough, a promising next step in his career.

The most pressing matter was finding a house, a search that quickly left him wanting. It's not that there was a shortage of available housing. On the contrary. But once he confessed to the size of his family, the place suddenly became unavailable. Nobody wanted to rent to a guy with eight kids. He'd talk by phone with Mary Lou every night and she only ever wanted to know what the holdup was. As George recalled, "She was going a little crazy, wanting to get out of Canada."

After a number of fruitless interviews with leasing agents, George finally met with an older woman named Frances Zerbey Braun who ran a music and art School at 607 Mahantongo Street in central Pottsville. Robert Braun had founded the Braun School of Music at Centre and Union Streets in 1912. During the mid-1930s, the school was moved to its present location at 607 Mahantongo Street. Mr. Braun died in 1955, and the school was then directed by his widow until 1969 when

Lawrence (Larry) Koch and his wife Marilu Amour Koch took ownership. Both the Kochs were noted performers and, as of this writing, continue to run the school today.

In 1964 Mrs. Braun also owned the house next door to the school at 605 Mahantongo Street and, though it had been vacant for some years and required considerable repair, the size of the house would be perfect.

After confessing to how many kids he had, George earnestly declared, "I promise, I'll do the entire restoration if you'll just rent it to me."

Mrs. Braun blanched at the size of his family. She had actually preferred not to rent the place at all, mostly for sentimental reasons, but George won her over. He could have the place. And thank goodness too because there really were no other options. Plus, for a house this size, the rent was very reasonable.

Mrs. Braun, however, had one very odd condition — George had to promise to "maintain the patina" on the bannister railing that ran three floors up the main stairwell. What with eight rambunctious kids constantly running up and down, the thing was almost certain never to acquire dust.

On his solemn vow that the railing would shine, the lease was signed.

Pennsylvania proved to be a genuine tonic for Mary Lou who, within a matter of weeks after the move, showed tremendous improvement. The steady gloom of Quebec was replaced by colorful sunlit hillsides. People not only spoke in a familiar tongue but did it with a smile. And most important of all, her children faced far more promising opportunities with better school systems. The climate was so much more agreeable, the language barrier had evaporated, and there were plenty of delightful friends to be made. Good shopping was still a ways away, but you can't have everything. All in all, the move had in many ways been a blessing.

The house at 605 Mahantongo Street was over 100 years old and hadn't been lived in for the past ten. There were numerous layers of wallpaper that had to be steamed away in practically every room, after which a good deal of replastering would need to take place. As was typical in a house of its age and stature, the kitchen was in the basement, a feature initially intended to keep servants out of sight during meal preparation and laundering. An ancillary benefit was that heat from the kitchen would rise to assist in warming the rest of the house and, with a family of ten, there was sure to be plenty of cooking.

Insulation was almost nonexistent, which didn't do much to keep the cold at bay. To regulate the house's main source of heat in cooler months, every room sported its own radiator, the entire system of which was fed by a city-operated common-feeder boiler that ran steam pipes to most every house in Pottsville — a network many decades past its prime. Such a large house with a big basement and three tall stories above required a considerable amount of heat. In the three-plus years the Cahill family lived in the drafty house on Mahantango Street, winters were always a fight for warmth.

Community steam feeder pipes ran under the streets, which helped keep many of the main thoroughfares from icing up in winter. The region was known for its sharp hills and streets, especially those close to downtown, with inclines averaging 30 degrees, though they seemed steeper. This made driving in any weather, particularly in winter, a challenge.

At over a hundred years old, the city's steam pipes constantly leaked and the main plant broke down a lot. This city-wide heating system had initially been touted as inexpensive because residents only paid for plant maintenance, a notion which, in recent decades, had become laughable.

The steam plant's boilers burned coal, the ash from which went up its chimneys and drifted down in a fine mist over the city. A microscopic dust of coal ash was everywhere, settling mostly over the city center, indoors and out. When the Cahills moved into the Mahantongo Street house they were met with a considerable cleaning job. A dull gray grime was everywhere, right down to the cracks in the floorboards.

When it snowed, instead of salting the streets, city trucks laid down coal cinders to lend vehicles traction, thereby avoiding the expense of road salt and taking advantage of a natural byproduct of the city's furnaces. The disadvantage of course was that, once the snow melted, the streets became a gritty gray muck.

The children attended St. Patrick's grade school that taught first-through-eighth grades. It was a mere 100 yards away on the opposite corner of the block, an easy three-minute walk from door to door.

The one Catholic high school in town, Nativity B.V.M. (Blessed Virgin Mary), was quite a bit further, situated atop a hill some four miles away past the city center and requiring a bus ride. Mary Lou was happy to once again have her children invested in the kind of quality education they'd recently been denied.

Though Pennsylvania winters could be problematic with temperatures often dipping below 30°F, the season was nothing compared to the brutal bitter gloom of Quebec. Pottsville had quite a bit more humidity and summers typically climbed to around 84°F. The climate overall was a tremendous improvement, sporting a full and glorious change of seasons.

Whenever Mary Lou had to shop she'd drive south about 35 miles down route 61 to Reading where Boscov's Department Store had most all the clothes and household goods she needed. Of course Boscov's had a wonderful restaurant in the store with the greatest pies and cakes. Mary Lou always treated herself there after shopping. And one of the kids always wanted to tag along to join her for one of those coveted meals.

The best and most affordable grocery stores were also in Reading, so a couple of times a month she would make the journey there to stock up on food stuffs for the troops.

On one such trip she locked the keys in the car and had to call George at the office. He left work with a company car and made the hour drive down and back to rescue her. As he walked up to unlock the car, she pulled out a little camera from her purse and snapped his picture. The look on his face was not pleasant. Even in times of great stress, Mary Lou had a knack for preserving the moments that cement a relationship. The photo is long gone. But George remembered fondly that, even when she embarrassed herself, Mary Lou would always flip the focus to that of a positive outcome, counting on his tolerance and his love.

The self-imposed task of cooking for an army, of committing one's self to years and years of the day-in-day-out scrounging up of meals for a demanding gaggle, this is a mad person's vocation, one not to be entered into without the armor of true devotion. And devotion it was, to food and to family.

From the perspective of one who's being fed, there's a real comfort and intimacy to a great recipe — a confident hand instructing one exactly how to proceed, and the promise of a satisfying result. That she cobbled together and squirreled away so vast an assembly of recipes for soups, stews and chili's, casseroles, cakes and collected concoctions, all built on a shoe string budget — it makes one marvel at Mary Lou's industrious nature, even some fifty years after the fact. She not only knew how to cook on a large scale, but to wholesomely nourish and deliberately delight, all while economizing at every turn. Meals in the Cahill house, never cheap but always thrifty, were a feast for the eyes and the soul, conceived, plotted and carried out with efficiency and aplomb.

Her creativity in the kitchen was legend in the family and her recipes roadmaps to healthful goodness. Brought up in a Great Depression and denied by the circumstance of her own youth, she carried with her vivid memories of deprivation, ever determined that her children would not suffer those same experiences.

Drawn in her formative years to fashion and design, Mary Lou's hunger was not only nutritional but intellectual. A meal, she firmly believed, ought not to be merely satisfying but delightful. An expanding variety of flavors and well rounded nutrition populated her ever expanding repertoire. Presentation was as much a part of any meal as nourishment. The sheer logistics of perfectly timing each aspect of a meal so that all its elements arrived almost simultaneously at the table — and piping hot! — was something akin to a small miracle. She conducted such a symphony every night without fail.

Of the many budget-trimming tricks up her sleeve, Mary Lou economized at every opportunity on so many little things, like milk. A family of ten consumed tons of the stuff. For every gallon of fresh milk purchased, she'd mix up a second gallon, adding water to powdered milk, and blend the two gallons to stretch those dollars. The resulting mixture tasted great and was probably one of the earlier instances of reduced fat milk. Bakeries typically discounted their day-old bread so she rarely bought fresh. She'd stock up in bulk and freeze the excess. She clipped all kinds of coupons and relied on money saving recipes like tuna casserole and Doctor Martin's Mix. Her home made spaghetti sauce was (and remains) a family favorite.

Breakfasts were healthy and varied. Cold cereal most of the year, occasionally pancakes or eggs, and hot breakfasts of oatmeal and a side of fresh stewed prunes in the winter months.

Evening meals only ever took place in the dining room at a neatly set table with clean table cloth or place mats, folded napkins, and properly placed flatware at every place setting.

Condiments with commercial labels were mostly forbidden on the table — proper salt and pepper shakers, sugar bowl and cream pitcher freshly filled, butter in a butter dish with butter knife, and, for spaghetti, Parmesan cheese in a bowl with serving spoon. Everyone lent a hand with Mary Lou issuing orders to fill the glasses, deliver hot serving dishes to the table, making certain to place iron trivets under each one so as not to scar the table, and sending a scout to call everyone down to eat, making sure to "Wash your hands for dinner!"

In the often drafty four-story house on Mahantango Street, permeating aromas of fresh fried chicken, pot roast and gravy, or that magnificent spaghetti sauce, would wend their way up the stairwells to every room, so that when a child's voice called out, "Dinner!", there sounded an immediate charge of feet.

Once seated, heads were bowed in unison followed by a light touch to the forehead, abdomen, shoulder and shoulder. Then came the recitation, "Bless us, oh Lord, and these thy gifts, which we are about to receive, from thy bounty, through Christ our Lord. Amen." Above all else, Mary Lou's children would honor the Catholic traditions that had been her salvation, instilled by the nuns of her youth.

Then began the mannered passing of serving dishes. If you didn't care for greens, too bad. Everyone had to eat some peas, string or Lima beans. Servings were carefully monitored. If food was placed on your plate, every single bite had to be eaten. "We do not waste food in this house."

Her own mother during the Great Depression in the 1930's had struggled to get food on her own table and had even bartered and bargained for meals on occasion, an experience that made Mary Lou ever grateful for any decent meal. She seized every opportunity to make her children aware that gratitude for a meal, however meager, was always required.

At the same time, why shouldn't a meal be a pleasurable experience? It didn't cost any more and it cultivated in her children a kind of social etiquette that would serve them well throughout their lives. Food just tasted that much better when it was handsomely served and manners were practiced. It was also her way of gifting her children with the very kinds of meals she'd only dreamed of as a little girl. Mary Lou remained staunchly determined that hunger would forever be a stranger in her home.

Politics and world affairs were rarely, if ever, discussed at dinner. Table conversation revolved mostly around school, chores or an upcoming holiday, all punctuated by the occasional game of 20 Questions. Family meals were carefully coordinated pleasant affairs, as well as one more opportunity to reinforce etiquette. No dinner was navigated without several calls of "Elbows off the table", "Sit up straight", "Chew with your mouth closed", "Help your sister with that", "Use your napkin" or "Don't talk with your mouth full."

The most popular exchange was, "What do we say?", prompting a "Please" or "Thank you."

"Can I leave the table?" was met with "*May* I leave the table? And yes, you may, after you clear your dishes."

Dinner wasn't dinner without dessert. Whether cake or ice cream, Jello or pudding, or even strawberry shortcake cobbled together by ladling defrosted frozen strawberries over a slice of angel food cake and topped with a button of whipped cream. Extras were well worth the effort. With a touch of creativity, pennies were stretched and bargains parlayed into banquets.

Mary Lou went to great lengths to make an evening meal a real affair. Once every month or so, a beautiful meat loaf with fresh whipped mashed potatoes and buttery green peas would appear. Or perhaps a lovely pot roast with onion roasted potatoes and cooked carrots. A creamy beef Stroganoff over a bed of noodles with French green beans was a favorite treat. Juicy pork chops with rice was a popular favorite. Or her special chili, famous spaghetti or pan fried chicken.

Holiday meals were the most extravagant affairs. A gigantic roast turkey with every conceivable trimming for Thanksgiving and Christmas made the dinner table a cover photo from Better Homes and Gardens magazine. Everyone was press-ganged into lending a hand; *very* carefully getting out the rarely used family china and crystal stemware; opening with reverence the polished wooden case, segmented in blue velvet compartments, housing the precious family silverware — all wedding gifts received in 1948 and all of which were brought out a couple times a year for only the best occasions.

The week, and weekend, prior to a holiday was employed cleaning the house top to bottom, ironing and laying out the holiday tablecloth and linen napkins, and checking off lists of food stuffs to be prepped with military precision, plus decorations to be hung or displayed. Everyone had carefully assigned chores. Laundering and ironing clothes to be worn for the celebration was completed. Even the right holiday record albums were carefully placed next to the family stereo so that all the most affecting Christmas music would be handy to top off the holiday mood. Nat King Cole, Perry Como, Andy Williams, the Percy Faith Orchestra, Hugo Montenegro and Mantovani collectively provided the soundtrack for these wholesome holidays.

Mary Lou was forever on the lookout for a new meal that could serve ten and not cost a fortune. Her bible was the Better Homes and Gardens cookbook to which she'd add her own twists to traditional meals as well as new recipes clipped from magazines as well as hand copied instructions with her own variation on a theme from a newspaper, a recommendation from a neighbor, or even a happy accident she'd stumbled upon while substituting something in the cupboard for an ingredient unavailable.

In following reliable recipes, she gradually assembled a tidy armory of spices and condiments to combat blandness at every turn. Whether dining out or cooking in, good food was a spiritual consideration for Mary Lou. An Easter ham was no mere hunk of meat. The extra expense of plugging half a jar of whole cloves into its rind and pinning it with juicy pineapple rings and a drizzle of honey elevated a holiday meal from pedestrian to euphoric.

Every child in the house had assignments, helping in the kitchen during preparation like peeling potatoes, taking biscuits out of the oven, tossing a salad, icing a cake. Even scrubbing pots and washing dishes, folding the table cloth and sweeping the floor afterwards.

"It's your turn to do the dishes. I did them last night", was a common exchange.

Mary Lou absolutely and utterly loved food. Having grown up with so little, it was the realization of a dream to not only provide good, healthy food for her own children, but to do it with flavor, variety and panache. That she managed it so magnificently and on such a minuscule budget for over 30 years is reason enough for canonization.

Peg Bracken's "I Hate to Cook" Cookbook along with her Better Homes & Gardens bible were the most dog-eared dialectics in her library, each one paper clipped with dozens of hand copied menu favorites collected from who-knows-where or scissored from an obliging "Ladies Home Journal" or "Woman's Day" magazine. Pages were well worn and butter stained, christened with coffee rings, and dusted with brown sugar, flower and baking soda. By example, all her children were taught to be capable hands in the kitchen.

"Don't ever expect a woman to be your servant," she told the boys. "Some of the world's greatest chefs are men."

She insisted each of her children learn to do their own laundry, ironing and mending, and to keep a clean house. All chores came with an inspection at the end and, if it was poorly executed or incomplete, it was to be repeated — but this time with efficiency. The lesson was: A lazy person works twice.

"Always take pride in what you do, however menial you think it may be," she would say again and again. "It builds character and a sense of accomplishment."

She encouraged her kids to find joy in whatever they did. Even the most detestable task can be made bearable if one treats it as a contest or game rather than a chore. In practicing what she preached, Mary Lou could often be caught singing to herself while working. Her playfulness and bubbly sense of fun was one of the very many endearing things about her.

Mary Lou Cahill was the finest practitioner of the manners she preached. Every command she gave was delivered with affection and encouragement. And always preceded by a "Please". Upon completion, a sincere compliment of a job well done was bestowed with a genuine "Thank you." Acknowledgement of any worthwhile effort was a big thing for her, whether a simple chore, a scholastic achievement, talent, or performance in a sport or school play.

And the active bolstering of self esteem out loud to the family during the evening meal was common practice: "Susan made tonight's dessert from scratch, measuring out all the ingredients, baking it and icing it all by herself and I think she did a marvelous job." Or "Christopher made all A's on his report card. We're so proud of your hard work."

Confidence building was a hallmark of George and Mary Lou's parenting practice. They had such pride in all their children individually. It was especially important that each child understood his or her value to them, and to the family, and every one was regularly held up as an example of accomplishment.

Projecting a positive attitude was also of principle concern to Mary Lou, who forever advocated a pleasant disposition in the face of hardship. Courtesy, kindness, tolerance and encouragement were hallmarks of her creed and were practiced in abundance.

Clothes for the kids were judiciously managed, often through hand-me-downs, with many garments seeing use by three or even four different children. New clothes were always purchased with durability in mind.

Speaking the language well was of special concern to Mary Lou, all part of her best-foot-forward regimen. Grammar was constantly being corrected, many times with an anecdotal addendum tacked on. Once, when asked about the difference between the two pronunciations of the word vase, Mary Lou responded, "Well, if it costs less than twenty five dollars, it's a '*Vace*' — and more than twenty five, then it's a '*Vozz*'", adding a roll of her eyes on the latter.

She was not an advocate of 'antiques'. For Mary Lou, a second hand store held many of the same treasures but at a far better value. In Pottsville, Larry Lumpkin's Junk Shop was her go-to destination. She loved to get old furniture, much of it not in the best shape, but always at a bargain. She'd bring each piece home in the station wagon and ask George, "Can you fix this?"

Of course, after a long day at work, he'd spend odd evenings stripping, painting, and bringing these treasures back to life for her. She had impeccable taste, spotting the potential in even the most neglected cabinet or chair. But that's how one furnishes a big house on a budget.

New purchases were rare, though George had always wanted a nice leather chair of his own. Their second year in Pottsville Mary Lou surprised him at Christmas with a beautiful new richly polished Cordova armchair with matching ottoman all trimmed up in brass studs. The king finally had a throne worthy of his station. He would spend many a night in that glorious chair hunkered down over his latest library book.

The Cahill's next door neighbors at 603 Mahantango St. were the Martins. Mr. Martin was the manager of the Pottsville Coca-Cola plant. His wife Cass Martin and Mary Lou became good friends and they'd occasionally visit or have coffee between household chores and errands.

George was well liked at Allied's Pottsville plant as the new assistant manager. His boss Guy Walters was a bit of a challenging personality, and not at his best when dealing with people. Though George had previously only dealt with chemicals, in Pottsville he now had to learn plastics. The facility's output primarily involved sheet film on rolls, such as the kind of plastic used by supermarkets to wrap meat products, as well as a number of other impressive plastic products. ACLAR was a great film that was impervious to just about any chemical including acid. For example, it was employed as a wrap for buoys to keep them from being degraded by salt water.

At the end of 1965 the Pottsville plant was also poised to produce a clear, heat resistant NYLON material, which, at the time, created a new international sensation — "Boil-in-a-Bag" food products. It's still in use today. The company was acquiring the process from an Italian firm. Since George oversaw all maintenance and engineering at the Pottsville plant, he would be supervising the installation of the new Italian system.

There was a plant in Milan, Italy that had mastered the operation. As part of their agreement to purchase the technology, George, along with five or six other guys, was sent over for six weeks to learn the operation.

And that's how, in January 1966, he took his first ever trip to Europe.

While training in Milan, Italian employees loved showing the Americans several key attractions and dining venues around the city, which George loved. On weekends the Milan plant would shut down so every Friday night George and another worker named Julie

Krushnick, an older fellow by about 12 years, would take a train together to explore other cities. Italian trains were a marvel of efficiency, always arriving and departing exactly on time and for very little money.

On one weekend excursion to Rome George and Julie stayed at a first class hotel. They'd breakfast and walk or take a bus to see the sights. That Sunday they saw a wedding going on and George decided to crash it.

Mr. Krushnick protested, "You can't do that. They'll throw you out."

So Julie stayed outside while George strolled on in, helping himself to a plate of good food and a nice cup of coffee, soaking up a bit of local color from all the vibrant personalities celebrating around him. No one minded or even questioned his presence. Eventually everyone lined up to kiss the bride. That's when George decided it was time to take his leave.

Two or three weeks into the training program with the Italians, Pottsville's plant manager Guy Walters decided to fly over and join his employees, checking on their progress. The locals took him out for the evening and introduced him to a fancy green drink. George hated it. But Guy was not a cautious drinker and downed several glasses of the green stuff becoming completely drunk. Back at the hotel Guy, looking very green himself, went up in the elevator just ahead of the group. When it returned and the doors opened, Guy had gotten off but the walls and floor of the car were drenched in great pools of the hideous green beverage. George complained to management that "somebody" threw up in the elevator. His estimation of his boss was not much improved after that.

On another evening out in Milan, George and Julie treated themselves to a performance at the legendary La Scala Opera House. George recalled their view of the luxurious horseshoe shaped theatre from their third tier center balcony seats as being the "most beautiful sight", all richly appointed in red velvet.

Walking home after the opera, a car eased up along side them with two cheerful Italian women offering their favors. Responding with a courteous wave and a "No thanks", George and Julie made their way back to the hotel.

George's weekend jaunts around the countryside exposed him to an Italy that he would be anxious to share with Mary Lou upon his return home, all supported by snapshots with stories of beautiful sites and wonderful food. And indeed she sparked right away to the idea of visiting Europe. The two of them enthusiastically made plans to travel there, though it would be another six years before they would make their first trip abroad together.

When Kathy graduated high school in 1967, she really wanted to do something special and chose the Air Force. She was the first of the children to leave home. After basic training, she was assigned to an intelligence group in Hawaii, identifying photo reconnaissance for bombing raids during Vietnam. Mary Lou and George were grateful their daughter was well away from the front lines of the conflict and Kathy seemed to thrive in an environment that trusted her capability with such sensitive information. At one point Mary Lou flew to Hawaii to stay with Kathy for a few weeks on a something of a vacation.

In April of 1967 George and Mary Lou had to once again pay quite a bit on income taxes, at which point Lou angrily declared, "You know what — we're going to *buy* a house so we can get the tax deduction."

On Sundays the two of them started driving around looking for places and discovered a new development on the southern edge of town called Forest Hills. The model houses appeared made to order and the Cahills signed a contract for a new construction. The house would be ready at the end of the year.

Mary Lou was never one for idling and was ever on the lookout for family activities. One weekend she rose early to whip up a great batch of fried chicken, packed it in a picnic basket with coleslaw and potato salad, filled a cooler with lemonade, and piled the family into the car for a trip to Washington, D.C. The the kids got to see the sites and ate a fried chicken lunch in the park. The Natural History Museum, Lincoln Memorial and the FBI building were toured and everyone took the elevator to the top of the Washington Monument, a spot George and Mary Lou had visited some 20 years earlier on their honeymoon.

Now and then day trips took the Cahills to local parks, driving to locks in upstate New York to see the ships go through, and most anything that was free and occupied the children's interest. Other weekend outings involved a pleasant drive in the Pennsylvania countryside perhaps stopping at a farmers market, an obliging roadside fruit stand or, best of all, visiting a dairy farm called Barn Hill's that served its own brand of ice cream directly adjacent to their own miniature golf course.

Summers of course usually meant overloading the station wagon with luggage, piling the kids in, and hitting the road for Florida. So used was she to seeing passing cars on the highway pull up beside them with someone inside counting to themselves while poking a finger in the Cahills' direction and calculating a sum, that Mary Lou would joke about wanting to hold up a handmade sign that read: *YES, 8!*

Renting a beach cottage at Indian Rocks Beach or Madeira Beach near Tampa, swimming and sunning for several weeks with Mary Lou and George's relatives, and then slogging back up to Pennsylvania — it was all part of the Cahill summer ritual.

Christmas holidays came and went in a blur at the end of 1967 and a few weeks later Mary Lou sent a four-page typed letter to her mother Mabel, who was now living in Indiana and feeling neglected. Here is the entire text of that letter:

January 20, 1968

Dear Mother,

No, we're not mad at you and nothing is wrong. So much has happened I don't know where to begin. We still haven't sent our Christmas cards or George's mother's gift yet. It's hectic enough just getting ready for Christmas with this bunch without moving at the same time.

Our house was supposed to be ready the middle of October but wasn't. George took the remaining two weeks of his vacation the last of November so we could move but the house still wasn't ready so he antiqued furniture and ordered the materials for finishing the fifth bedroom for the boys. Two days before he had to go back to work, the house was ready. He was able to almost finish the boys' room except for the closet and the floor. We moved a few things over and started cleaning the place the first weeks in December but the weather was starting to get bad and he had to go out of town on business a couple of times so that delayed things. It was getting so close to Christmas that I wanted to stay in the other house and have Christmas there although everyone else was gung-ho to get in the new place. I just about had everyone convinced that that was the best thing to do when the steam heat in the old house was off for 48 hours straight. The steam company kept saying the heat would be on any time. Finally George said there was heat in the new house so at 2 o'clock on the morning of December 17th he, George, Sue, Mike and Chris put the beds in the truck George had borrowed from the plant while I got the pajamas and clothes together for all of us. Naturally with the beds here we had to stay here so George and the boys started moving all the rest of the furniture over the next day. I hadn't done any Christmas shopping yet and I had to get Kathy's things mailed.

Mike, Chris, Mary and Deb take the school bus to school now but George and Sue have to ride with me when I drive Lisa to kindergarten. Lisa used to walk. It was so close to our old place and she loves it and is learning a lot so I hadn't the heart to tell her she couldn't go anymore since we were moving. I take her in the morning and pick her up at 11:15 every day. Besides all that, this year was the first year Debbie was picked to be in the Christmas program at school and I just couldn't tell her she couldn't be in it, so I had to get her an outfit together and look all over for red velvet ribbon for a sash for her white dress and her hair. Then George had the lead in "Arsenic and Old Lace" put on by the drama club at school a week before Xmas, so that meant I had to take the Sunday afternoon I had intended to write letters and cards and go see him instead. He was excellent in the part and I enjoyed it but it was very bad timing since it put me even further behind.

Besides all the moving and Christmas the darnedest things keep happening to me. For instance, the morning after we moved over here getting everyone off to work and school was more hectic than usual since clothes couldn't be found and kids had to catch the school bus on time and others had to be driven. All in all I was one jump ahead of a fit by the time everyone was deposited. I decided to stop in a coffee shop and have some coffee and toast and regain my sanity and straighten out my yard long list of things I had to do. I had taken two bites of toast and a sip of coffee when I remembered I had two cents in my purse as I had given the kids all my money for lunches and milk. I didn't even have a dime for the phone. I asked the waitress if there was a phone I could use to call my husband to come bail me out and she said there was one in the kitchen. While I was calling George (who thought it was very funny), the cook kept trying to give me 35 cents. I thanked him and assured him my husband would be right over. George said he was busy and that it would be about 20 minutes before he could make it, so another cup of coffee and 45 minutes later he got there. I hadn't accomplished anything on my list and it was almost time to pick up Lisa so the composure I had sought to regain was shattered even more.

The next day I was over at the old house getting a few things and cleaning. I told Lisa to get her coat and hat on as we were going home. Our neighbor stopped by to see if I needed any help and Lisa said something and went outside. I thought she was waiting out in front but when I went out she was nowhere in sight. I called and called her and looked all over and at her girlfriend's house. Our neighbor was looking too. I got in the car and drove up to the candy store and school yard and asked a couple of people if they had seen a little girl fitting her description. I decided to go to her kindergarten room and if she wasn't there I was going to call the police. As I drove by our old house our neighbor stopped me and said Chris (he was home sick that day) had just phoned her and said Lisa had just walked in our house and wondered if I knew where she was. She had walked about three miles to our new place. I was so glad she was alright. She didn't know she had done anything wrong, she was so proud of herself, the first thing she said was, "I walked home all by myself." After I talked to her she was sorry she had scared me and promised never to do that again.

There was also the morning I was going to get a lot done after I dropped everyone off. When I got back home I discovered I didn't have the house key so had to go to the plant and get George's. When I got back it was almost time to pick up Lisa.

Yesterday morning I let Lisa off at the school. A couple of dogs that had followed kids to school were in the school yard. One of them went up to Lisa and playfully took her mitten off her hand. She couldn't get it back so I got out to help her. The mutt was playing with it and I couldn't get it, then this Collie came up and got the mitten, I couldn't get it from him either. The two of them were having one heck of a good time throwing it up in the air and tugging at it. They ran down the street and across the square while Lisa was crying. I told her not to cry, I'd get her mitten back or buy her new ones. She went on in and I got in the car and tried to locate the dogs. I drove around several blocks without seeing them, then I spotted one and then the other in the next block. I circled the block but they didn't have the mitten with them, then about four blocks from the school I saw this bright red mitten on top of a bare bush outside a shoe store and stopped and got it. It was a little dirty and slobbered on but that's all. I've said it before and I'll say it again "Blondes don't have more fun, mommies do!!"

Right now I'm behind in the mending, ironing, etc., and trying to make drapes for this house and put things in a permanent place plus keep up the daily routine of clean clothes and meals. Right now I've got to go over to the old place and help George get the rest of the things out of there and finish cleaning that place. All that boils down to the reason I haven't had time to write anyone.

We tried all day Christmas to call you but couldn't get a line through. Also tried a couple of times since, but no answer.

We got the lovely candles and they were our main Christmas decoration besides the tree. The girls were thrilled with their stand out petticoats and Sue loves the cute pink checked nightie. It was all divided so everyone got something. Thanks, everything was appreciated, especially the candles.

Kathy graduated from Intelligence School January the 16th. She is supposed to come home the end of this month, don't know the exact date yet, for a month. Then she's going to Hawaii for two years. She really seems to like it and has had three promotions in the six months she's been in.

George III still wants to go into oceanography. He's trying for all the scholarships available.

All of us are well except for the occasional cold. I'll try to write more often, I know I should do better. The road to hell is paved with good intentions and it looks like I'm well on my way. If I could latch on to a purchasing agent, cook, laundress, wardrobe mistress, chauffeur and housekeeper I'd be in good shape.

I got a letter from Helen before Christmas and have been trying to get a chance to write her too. Write and let us know how you are getting along. Remember, you always have a home with us any time you want it. We all love you and wish we could live closer. I'll drop you a letter next week and continue with more adventures of the Impossibles vs. the Super Heroes. (The kids vs. us!) It's a struggle, but the Super Heroes are winning.

All our love,

Lou, George & "Angels"

George III was the next to graduate high school and stated a preference for oceanography / underwater demolition, hoping to join the navy. He recalled his father's response: "What goes up must come down. But what goes down doesn't always come up." George III took this to heart, reconsidered his options and, after testing well for electronics, chose to enter the U.S. Air Force instead where he'd be assigned to avionics maintenance.

In 1971 after high school, Susan volleyed to be the first of Mary Lou and George's children to go to college and enrolled in Penn State University.

During his ten years in Pottsville, George was always open for promotion and worked his way incrementally up to Assistant Plant Manager. His boss, Guy Walters, was very ambitious, always pushing for a corporate promotion of his own, but he had a poor reputation for dealing with those under his command. George recalled an instance where another employee, who happened to be the son of one of the company V.P.'s, was unfairly targeted by Guy. The employee was a short fellow, very round and very sweet. But for some reason Guy just hated him and constantly gave him a hard time in front of other employees. He'd assault the fellow with petty grievances, yelling things like, "Take you hands out of your pockets!"

There was no sense to it.

Guy was never good interacting with people. He knew the mechanical end of plant operations well but that appeared to be his only strength.

On one occasion, George Jr. and George III ventured out on a Saturday for a game of golf and invited the V.P.'s son to join them. At one point the little guy hit his ball up a steep incline. Without hesitation, he earnestly struggled up the hill, spotted his ball, swung hard, and missed. The swing actually took him off his feet and the little fellow rolled all the way down the hill. It was flat out the funniest thing

George ever saw, but father and son did a good job pretending not to have seen it. Yet it had to be an incredibly humiliating experience for this luckless little guy.

Some years later, while touring a series of mansions in New England, Mary Lou and George happened to run into the same fellow, this time with his wife. They greeted each other warmly. He was still a very nice man and George always looked fondly on the sweet soul who'd done nothing to merit the shabby treatment he'd received from Guy Walters.

Each year Allied Chemical's plant managers had to complete personnel evaluations for each employee, filing reports with the company's headquarters in Morristown, New Jersey. By the early 1970's Allied had established a computerized system to keep track of these performance reports, breaking them down and ranking key qualifications. From this database the company developed a process for reaching out with promotion opportunities to ideal candidates.

Thanks to this new system, in the spring of 1973 George received a direct message from Allied's home office in New Jersey. He called immediately to confirm that yes, he was indeed interested in moving up, a sentiment he'd expressed repeatedly to every manager he'd ever worked under. After confirming an appointment to travel to Morristown for an interview, he informed Guy Walters of the offer.

Guy was visibly displeased.

It seems a previous fault in Allied's process had been that, when approaching an employee with a job offer, headquarters would contact, not the employee but rather their manager to ask if the candidate was interested in a promotion. Not long after taking up his new duties at the Morristown facility, George was informed that, "several times" prior to the offer he'd just accepted, Guy Walters had been contacted with job offers for George — all of which Guy promptly and repeatedly turned down, declaring George was not interested. And none of which he'd ever told George about.

After many of these attempts, corporate had been left with the impression that George would never be interested. It was only after the personnel department's computer system bypassed management and start messaging offers directly to employees that Guy Walters' charade was finally uncovered.

Of course, when she learned of Guy's deceit of many months, possibly years, Mary Lou was outraged. George himself was stunned that he'd been the victim of such a callous manipulation to intentionally stunt his own advancement within the company.

Any reasons for which Guy Walters repeatedly kept these offers from George can only be presumed, though it was widely known at the Pottsville plant that Mr. Walters himself had long been angling for a promotion of his own to company headquarters in New Jersey. While it was George who was ultimately recognized for his fine work and personable nature, after Guy's cruel charade was uncovered, the two men never saw or spoke to each other again.

Mary Lou would remark over the years that this was when she fell in love with computers because it was Allied's conversion to them that finally revealed George's having been passed over for promotions.

Some months after the Cahills left Pottsville, management at Allied Corporate executed what they called a "lateral arabesque" and transferred Guy Walters to a smaller facility in the south, practically the exact opposite of the promotion he'd always desired. Eighteen months later, Guy's secretary heard a commotion and a crash in his office. When she entered, Guy was on the floor by his desk, the victim of a fatal heart attack.

12

Morristown

The Cahills packed up and sold the house at 94 Deerfield Drive in Pottsville, only to have George purchase a suitable house at 33 Deerfield Road in Whippany, New Jersey, a suburb of Morristown where Allied Chemical's Corporate headquarters was situated. Perhaps there was something magical in any street with "Deerfield" in its name.

New Jersey, being a mere 45 minutes from New York City, meant George and Mary Lou could take full advantage of theatres, museums and world class restaurants, all just a train ride away. They went into "the city" as often as they could manage, which was wonderful.

Allied's Morristown campus consisted of several departments. George was in the General Chemical Division with the title Director of Maintenance and Engineering. In brief, the job entailed traveling to a wide variety of Allied plants to bring them up to date on best practices for maintenance, including improvements right there at company headquarters. About this time all company facilities had just finished being computerized and two of the young men in George's department were pretty savvy at programming so he had them convert all maintenance blueprints over to computerized data that could be pulled up on screens for broader, faster access.

A Vice President had once told George: "If you're going to be a good manager, you have to be a little bit of an S.O.B.", a philosophy he came to appreciate. While George ever remained personable and pleasant, he understood and embraced the practice of not being too chummy with personnel he may one day be required to reprimand or even fire. He strove to maintain a pleasant posture of respect for, yet appropriate distance from, the people he supervised.

Even at his home facility in Morristown, there were always some for whom George's managerial decisions (necessary though they were) represented unwelcome change. Whenever he instituted an improvement, down through the ranks his fiats were unflatteringly declared to be "DAP decisions" (Dictatorial, Arbitrary and Priggish) inferring they were made cavalierly and based on limited information, which was never the case.

Example: Shortly after arriving in Morristown, George discovered an inordinate amount of motor fuel was being consumed by the facility's trucks; in particular, by a large number of pickup trucks, which were employed for driving around the campus. Each of the seven maintenance foremen had his own pickup truck. If they had to go 100 feet from one building to another to check a meter, they'd use the pickup truck. George made a command decision that when these trucks wore out, which they shortly did, he would not replace all of them. The maintenance foremen were incredulous. "How are we supposed to get around the site?"

"I'll get you bicycles."

The foremen were extremely unhappy with this outrageous call and loudly registered their complaints, even though they eventually got used to it, perhaps even benefitting from a bit of mild exercise. Literally thousands of dollars in vehicle maintenance and fuel costs instantly went away.

Later, when George learned many employees were making as much in overtime as they were for regular hours, he announced that henceforward all overtime would first need to be approved by him. Overtime plunged. Again complaints were numerous. Overtime? Bicycles? And this was while he was head of just one department — Maintenance and Engineering.

Management took notice.

At Allied's annual summary meeting, each department made a short presentation to the company's CEO. One after another, managers wrote on a white board a couple of words to do with productivity, then offered a few comments about procedures and quotas.

When George stood up, he put the white board to good use, listing every departmental concern with bullet points and examples, illustrating challenges, proposals, team input, potential solutions and procedures. He summed up with a list of actions and consequences relating to efficiency, savings, employee morale and productivity. It was a concise and well-articulated snapshot of a department whose team (and leader) had a firm grasp of problem solving, and an even firmer grasp of how a well-oiled department ought to operate.

Again, management took notice.

During his first year there, George Cahill reduced the facility's maintenance costs by a cool one million dollars.

It was Autumn 1974 when the two of them finally took their very first journey together abroad, flying to Italy and introducing Mary Lou to the marvels she and George had discussed at length since his return from Milan six years earlier. She finally understood what he'd been raving about all along. Of course the trip was magical for both of them and only served to whet their appetite for more.

At this point five of their children were still living at home. By the end of 1974, Michael and Chris had both tried their hand at college while Mary and Deb were continuing on at Whippany Park High School. By '75 Chris turned to computer programming for an insurance company. Michael bowed out of college as well and headed out on his own, landing in Kansas. By this time Susan had gotten married and had a baby, as well as Kathleen who, a couple of years earlier after completing her Air Force service, had also married and had a child.

Though the move to Morristown had meant a boost in responsibility for George, it demanded a good deal of travel, which took him away from his family more than he'd have wished. To supplement the their income, Mary Lou had been working a part time job as an interviewer for the National Opinion Research Center. Now with fewer children at home, she decided to rejoin the workforce full time. When Lisa, her youngest, started high school in 1976, Mary Lou went to work for Bergen Brunswig Drug Company as a switchboard operator and receptionist. In 1979 she was promoted to personal secretary for two of the company's vice presidents. Then in May of that year she transitioned to being a representative for the drug division, at which time she also enrolled in Fairleigh Dickenson University to study advertising principles in sales and marketing. These studies, combined with her innate savvy, paid off.

The sales reps in Bergen Brunswig's drug division, all of whom happened to be men, only allowed her to pursue the dregs of their client list — pharmacies that rarely, if ever, stocked the company's products. Undaunted, Mary Lou charmingly wondered aloud to these independent drug store owners that, as a woman who relied on pharmacies for so many conveniences, why did they not stock products that she used, that every woman used, and used often? With over 30 years experience getting children to do what was best for them, Mary Lou turned around these shop owner's thinking on women's products, which the men in her company hadn't understood and mostly ignored. Previously resistant pharmacists were suddenly placing orders larger than any of her fellow sales reps had seen.

In the nine years she worked at Bergen Brunswig, Mary Lou thoroughly enjoyed herself. A pharmacist once asked her how she liked working.

"I've always worked", she responded. "But I sure like getting paid for it now."

Unexpectedly George's dear mother Mae passed away on August 22, 1980 and George and Mary Lou traveled to Florida to attend her funeral. Her passing deeply affected George. Her sound discipline, sturdy work ethic, and warm and cheery disposition had always been a touchstone for the compassion and wisdom that guided his own life. She had survived four husbands, raised three marvelous daughters and one magnificent son.

Later that year the Senior Vice President in charge of all Allied operations in Morristown called George late in the day and said, "I want to see you right away. Right now."

George was heading into the VP's office just as his own boss, Hal, Director of Facilities and Services, was coming out. Hal was white as a sheet and hurried past without looking at George.

Inside the Sr. VP got right to it.

"George, you're being promoted to Director of Facilities and Services."

"What about Hal?"

There was an uncomfortable pause.

"He's a nice guy but doesn't have operations experience at plant level."

"Then what's Hal doing?"

"Retiring."

"When?"

"Now."

Stunned by the suddenness of it, George went back to his office and sat down to wrap his head around it when he noticed it was 4:30. The day was over.

In the car on his way home, George happened to notice Mary Lou also driving home from Bergen Brunswig and signaled her to pull over. They stopped in a nearby parking lot and when she joined him in his car, seeing the stunned look on his face, she'd suspected the worst. But the news was wonderful for them.

As new Director of Facilities and Services for all of Morristown's operations, George's responsibilities suddenly expanded exponentially. With this promotion, and the money that came with it, the notion of affording a real retirement started to seem less distant.

At Bergen Brunswig Mary Lou did a lot of work with the head of the company. He liked her a lot and knew she hadn't worked long enough to qualify for their pension program. One day he came to her and asked, "Do you have any stock in the company?" She didn't. He quietly wondered if maybe she wouldn't want to buy some. Apparently something was about to happen and Mary Lou took the hint. She took some bonus money she'd saved and bought a block of company stock at about $8.00 a share. Very shortly the market registered a big change in the company and the stock jumped quite a bit. She continued to hang onto that stock and over the years it split two or three times paying out some nice dividends. As of June 2022 Bergen's stock was valued at over $144.00 a share and was still growing.

Mary Lou had actually been planning to retire from Bergen Brunswig in 1987 but Allied Chemical merged with Signal Corporation in late 1985 and the newly named Allied Signal found they suddenly had too many people on their payroll. The company decided to divest itself of excess personnel across the board by 10 percent. George worked closely with his boss, a Vice President, to look at his own group for reasonable cuts.

Rather than see anyone fired, George chose to approach people to whom Allied could offer an early retirement package. Then, after looking at all jobs company wide, and realizing there were simply too many levels of management between the president and the lowest salaried positions, he even recommended that his own job be eliminated entirely. Management took his recommendations to heart and, in June of 1986, George's bosses hit him with a surprising proposal: "If you retire right now, we'll still pay your full salary for the next year — after which you'll be put on full pension."

With their last child Lisa having just graduated college, and all their other children making their own ways in the world, there was no reason to continue working. With very little discussion Mary Lou and George took Allied up on its offer. They both retired immediately.

It was July 1986.

13

Sunshine, Here We Come!

Faced with selling the house at 33 Deerfield Road in Whippany, George had some rough dollar estimates in mind. He'd done his research and established the property's value compared to other houses in the neighborhood. He consulted three different realtors, two of whom came back with good, respectable offers. But one woman returned with an appraisal figure far above anything George and Mary Lou imagined. After deciding to go with this last realtor, the house sold quickly and at the exact price the she'd predicted.

With the sale finalized, it took Mary Lou all of ten seconds to decide to let go of (almost) all their New Jersey home's contents. They would purchase completely new furniture once they moved, resigning only a few important items to storage, including George's much loved leather chair. They then laid out a good portion of the proceeds from the Deerfield Road sale toward the price of a new home in Safety Harbor, Florida, which permitted them to maintain only a small mortgage. Over the next several months they waited out construction of their dream house from a rented condo in nearby Clearwater Beach, all the while working with a decorator to make certain their sparkling new decorations and furnishings were ready for them the moment they moved in on May 6, 1987.

Prior to moving to Florida Mary Lou had never seriously invested herself in golf. George told her she would enjoy it and should learn. As a lifelong aficionado, George's sister Mary Nutting also encouraged Mary Lou to take up the game. So she and George joined the Safety Harbor country club, enjoying all its perks and amenities. Though Mary Lou was not a long ball player, according to George she turned into a good short drive golfer, a fine chipper and an excellent putter. The Cahills ended up playing a great deal of golf over the years and, as a pair, entered a good number of tournaments where they did very well.

On one occasion at the club, George and Mary Lou were asked if two men could join them for a foursome. On the 2nd hole Mary Lou hit a nice drive just short of the hole. Then strolled on up, casually chipped it and, even as she started walking toward the green, the ball rolled right into the hole. These two guys said, "Wow."

With a secret delight George casually snapped back, "Oh, she does that all the time."

During one golf vacation in France they stayed at a sister resort to their club in Florida, enjoying a really good rate. One day Mary Lou was playing with George on a par 4 hole. She drove her ball to within spitting distance of the green. Some German women were watching from the side when Mary Lou chipped her second shot up onto the green and very close to the hole. The women clapped enthusiastically and declared her a master, to which she responded with a celebratory wiggle.

Mary Lou and George had worked incredibly hard for many years to build a life, raise a family, and distance themselves from the hardships of their respective youths. In so doing they'd developed a unique talent for heralding the successes of others and demonstrating on a regular basis how very important it was to value and celebrate family. In all her years as a wife and mother, Mary Lou was steadfast in her tracking of key family events, christenings, graduations, and holidays. Only in extreme circumstances did she ever miss sending birthday and Christmas cards and gifts, especially to her children and grandchildren.

As for Allied Signal, the company would call George back a couple of times to testify in age discrimination cases associated with the mass retirements. But there had been no discrimination and the cases were all dismissed. He finally told Allied, "Please don't call me for these anymore. I'm retired."

Mabel Rominger's last marriage to the band leader Clyde Gardner hadn't lasted very long. Afterward she proceeded to bounce around the country and, aside from living with the Cahills in Cleveland for a few years in the late 1950's, she didn't always stay in touch with her children. Though Mary Lou attempted to keep up with her mother through letters, gifts and cards, Mabel remained elusive, ever the gypsy, the wandering soul, sometimes here, sometimes there. By the early 1980's she had gravitated back to Indiana, landing not far from her parents' farm near Paoli and operating a flower shop. Helen would always be close, if not right by her side.

Sometime around 1986 or so, Helen contacted Mary Lou. Mabel was not faring well, troubled by arteriosclerotic heart disease and bouts of dementia. Helen had no money so Mary Lou worked to find a suitable facility that would best tend to Mabel's needs. She paid for her mother's care at the Jasper Nursing Center and, over the next few years, visited regularly and continued to write. It was difficult for Mary Lou during her last several visits, to sit holding a smile, as Mabel wagged a finger at her, asking Helen, "Who is that?"

Artist, actor, fashion designer, sculptor, singer, fighter and ferocious defender of education, renovator, builder, firebrand, and beloved mother of two phenomenal children, Mabel Claudine Evelyn Rominger Sayles died of a pulmonary embolism in Jasper, Indiana on Sunday the 13th of March 1988. Her son Jean Sayles traveled from his farm in Lebanon, New Hampshire and stood with his sister Mary Lou Cahill as the two of them laid their mother's ashes to rest in the frozen ground of Ames Chapel Cemetery, not far from her father Perry Everett Rominger, but closer still to her mother Cena May Bostock.

At long last Mabel was at peace.

One of Mary Lou's most profound losses was that of her beloved Aunt Helen, the dear sweet woman who practically raised her (along with Mabel). Helen succumbed to cardiomyopathy in the late winter of 1997 and passed away at Memorial Hospital on the morning of Thursday January 23rd. Mary Lou and George traveled to Indiana to pay their respects, again at Ames Chapel Cemetery. Helen Marjorie Rominger was buried close to her darling sister and lifelong partner-in-crime, Mabel Rominger. Helen was 87.

Jean Sayles had said goodbye to his beloved 130 acre farm in Lebanon, New Hampshire and retired to the warmth of Tucson, Arizona with his darling wife Dorothy. After a marvelous life together for 59 years of marriage, and having raised three magnificent children — Mark, Lynne, and Elizabeth — on Thursday October 22, 2009 Francis Harvey "Jean" Sayles passed away.

He was 88.

Mary Lou was particularly affected by the loss of her dear brother. Jean had been her protector, champion and best friend throughout her childhood and she carried his influence with her all her life. His loss was too sudden and incredibly sad for her.

Jean and Dorothy's son Mark delivered the eulogy at his father's memorial and his words painted an apt and loving portrait of a devoted and dedicated husband, father, and brother:

The Things My Father Loved

When we, his children, tried to think of the words that best describe our father, they all had the same ring — gentle, soft-spoken, mild-mannered, quiet. Quiet may be the best. He was quiet about his past, about growing up without a father, quiet about living a street urchin's life while his mother earned her livelihood in the traveling theater. He was quiet about the sacrifices he made to get an education, quiet about fighting for his country in World War II, quiet about his achievements as a professional civil engineer, quiet in his determination to provide for his children a comfortable, middle-class life — giving them the camps, lessons, and vacations that he never had as a kid.

He had a quiet sense of humor. He had a quiet way with words. He quietly loved the same woman for six decades. He quietly bragged about his children. He quietly cheered the underdog in any sporting event. He was even quiet in the kitchen — probably the only man on the planet who could make coffee and burn toast without a sound.

But quiet men often do remarkable things in quiet ways. My father designed and built large earthen and concrete dams in this country. He won a patent for an invention that made it possible to build the Alaska pipeline on permafrost. He worked in inhospitable places like Greenland, Siberia, and the Canadian arctic. At the height of the Cold War, he was one of the first American research civil engineers to visit the Soviet Union to study the problem of building dams on frozen soil. And his research in soil mechanics was published extensively in engineering and scientific journals.

And he went quietly about enjoying life too. He bought an old farmhouse in New England with a hundred acres of land — this with the purpose of raising his kids in the country. He spent every weekend and many nights quietly fixing up this old house with the help of free labor from his children. While fixing up this farmhouse Francis Sayles went quietly about teaching his children important lessons — the value of thrift, the virtue of self-reliance, and the joy of installing sheetrock, painting the porch, and cutting firewood over watching televised football on Saturday afternoons.

And then there was his vegetable garden — a source of quiet pride for my father. It was a rocky, hillside plot that my dad plowed and planted every year. He grew Swiss chard and pole beans, sweet corn and Big Boy tomatoes. Strawberries and zucchini. Lots of zucchini. His garden produced more zucchini than our family could eat, freeze, or even give away — though, that didn't keep my dad from trying. On summer mornings before going to the office, he loaded the family station wagon with zucchini — always the big ones, the ones you needed two hands to hold — and he took these to work with him. Now, my father knew better than to take zucchini into his office to give away. He had done that so many times that, when his co-workers saw him walking the hallways with arms full of zucchinis looking for places to leave them, they tactfully avoided him. So my father didn't take zucchini into the office. Instead he took them into the office parking lot. This was the 1960's and 70's. This was small town New Hampshire in the summer. The men my father worked with were civil engineers who drove Nashes and Ramblers and Jeeps to work — men who trustingly left their car doors unlocked and the windows rolled down in the office parking lot. And there went Francis Sayles, stopping his zucchini-loaded station wagon next to the open-widowed sedans of his co-workers, dropping zucchinis onto the driver's seat, moving on the next — quietly, of course — because even when it came to getting rid of zucchini, my father was quiet. Eventually his fellow engineers — "zucchini victims", he called them — learned to roll up their windows and lock their doors before Francis Sayles showed up in the office parking lot on summer mornings.

At heart, my father was a country boy. He loved growing his own vegetables, picking apples from his own orchard. He loved long walks on back roads — even in the middle of New England winters — and always with a dog. He loved cutting his own firewood to heat his house, plowing his driveway with his own tractor — it was a long driveway and an old tractor. He dug his own septic system, repaired his own cars, and made his own, hand-churned ice cream every fourth of July. The fact is, hand-churned ice cream was on my father's mind right until the end. Even in his last days, he ate ice cream at almost every meal!

His life, while full of struggles, was in the end a full and accomplished one — as a courageous soldier, as a well-educated professional, an expert in his field, as a loving husband, a devoted family man, and just a great dad. He will be remembered by those who knew him and loved him as the gentle, gracious, caring, quiet man who, though walked softly, left deep footprints in all of us.

We love you, Dad, and will try to spend our days in honor of your life.

At home in Safety Harbor, the Cahills found their greatest ease at their country club, playing and dining there frequently. In 1999 George invited about 50 or 60 people to the club to celebrate Mary Lou's 70th birthday. And again in 2009 most all the Cahill family and extended family journeyed to Florida to bid her a happy 80th.

Mary Lou and George stayed in the Safety Harbor house almost 14 years, enjoying its spacious ranch-style layout and beautiful screened-in pool. It was a perfect home base where Mary Lou cooked and planned travels abroad while George raised orchids and indulged in shooting and editing video. They were both accomplished and prolific photographers, collecting throughout their lives the most beautiful images of people and places they loved. If there was a smile to be coaxed or a sparkle in someone's eye, Mary Lou would whip out her little pink camera and capture the moment.

In 2001, George and Mary Lou elected to let go of their roomy home to build a more manageable place in Heritage Springs Retirement Village about 15 miles to the north in Trinity. The Safety Harbor house sold easily in a week's time, and at a handsome profit, which allowed them to pay cash for their new build. The Trinity place was to be an airy one-story duplex that the realtor called a "connected villa" in a gated community, ideally situated directly on a Golf Course. Of the sites available for new housing at the time, they had their pick of any plot near the course's sixth hole.

Ever the engineer, and having played the game extensively for so many years, George understood too well that people were not always the most capable golfers. Prior to picking a site for their new home, he and Mary Lou asked to be taken to the tee for the sixth hole. From there George pulled out his best wood and drove several balls as far down the fairway as he could, a respectable 150 yards or so. They then went to the ball that had traveled the furthest, just short of the green. George immediately pointed to the next plot beyond and declared, "*That's* where we want to build."

During their time in that lovely little Trinity villa, every single house between theirs and the tee filed insurance claims for glass damage. Even though George and Mary Lou would occasionally find a ball in their back yard, never once did they suffer a broken window from a golf ball.

Talk about resale value.

Back in 1972, on the occasion of his 50th birthday, George's daughter Kathleen had given him a travel diary. The inscription inside read:

"DADDY, HAPPY 50TH AND 50 MORE TO COME"

It took two more years, but in 1974, when he was finally able to put the diary to use on his first trip to Italy with Mary Lou, he chronicled each day's activities, a habit he would continue for years. Every time he and Mary Lou traveled abroad, George would keep a diary for the trip.

The two of them had returned home from that first Italian vacation with not enough pictures and more than enough plans to travel again soon. Over the next 36 years, the Cahills would visit England, Greece, Turkey, Jamaica, Scotland and Russia. They would also return to their beloved Italy five more times, but France held the top spot with a record 13 visits, each trip lasting anywhere from two to four weeks.

Their final sojourn abroad together was from September 1st through the 23rd in 2010, driving the French countryside, indulging in Mary Lou's favorite foods and wines. A month after their return, Mary Lou and George were rested enough to brave the chill of Chicago for a family Thanksgiving celebration.

There was so much for which to be thankful.

For some months Mary Lou had been fighting a very slight but naggingly persistent cough, though she'd kept it under control enough to enjoy her travels. Following the 2010 holidays her condition worsened and she was ultimately diagnosed with Pulmonary Fibrosis. Through much of February she was treated in earnest and in early March her breathing showed improvement enough to find a measure of relief and a return home.

On the first day of Spring 2011, a leisurely Sunday afternoon, Mary Lou was at home with George. After chatting with one of her children, she hung up the phone and was suddenly unable to breathe. George called an ambulance and Mary Lou was rushed to the hospital.

Her doctor greatly regretted telling George that complications of pneumonia and sepsis had set in. Mary Lou was on a respirator and unresponsive. There was little to be done. The children were notified and all but Kathleen and Michael were able to be there the next day to say goodbye.

George kissed the love of his life one last time and he and Mary Lou parted ways.

It was Monday March 21st, 2011.

She was 81, happily married for almost 62 years, and had lived wholeheartedly the career she'd always wanted, as that of a wife and mother.

A few years earlier, while making arrangements for this eventuality, Mary Lou and George hadn't given much thought to where in the cemetery they might prefer to reside. At first she thought anywhere would be fine but then, as they were about to leave the offices at Trinity Memorial Gardens, Mary Lou asked, "Do you have something under a tree?"

They did.

A double plot was reserved. Matching bronze plaques were installed with names and birth dates. No one could have anticipated the day another date would be added.

In the days after her funeral, George recalled that, in her lifetime, Mary Lou had harbored three great desires. The first was to visit Jerusalem. Political climates being what they were, this never came to pass. The second was to fly on the SST (Super Sonic Transport). Sadly, the last SST was retired before she got the chance. And lastly, to see the Pope — the one dream she achieved during a visit to Rome on Sunday October 4th, 1981.

George found it lovely that his wife's highest desires were to be close to the head of the church, visit the holy land, and skirt the stratosphere.

He had never known anyone in such a hurry to get to heaven.

Snapshots

Thomas Joseph Cahill (circa 1898)

Thomas and Blanche with daughters
Bessie (R) and Dorothy "Burb" (1907)

George Sr. with Mae, Mary, Carolyn and George Jr. — the only time the entire Cahill family was photographed together, as Mae was pregnant with Betty at the time (Jacksonville Beach 1926)

Mary, Carolyn and George Jr. (1928)

Mary and Betty Cahill (Detroit 1938)

George Jr., Butch Hardwick, Mary & Don Nutting (NY 1939)

George with his new 1941 Plymouth Deluxe Sedan

George visits his mom during shore leave (Detroit 1943)

Dear Folks,

Well I'm about to be drafted so I decided I better join the navy. Daddy used his enfluence and got me a rating Seaman, First Class, I am sending this so you can sign it Mom. If I had not joined the Navy they would have drafted me because they sent me my papers yesterday. When you get this go to a Notary Public and sign them in front of him. Let him put his seal on it, Soon as you get it send it back air mail, Special delivery. because I have a chance to get in a company down at Mayport and

The first page of a letter George Jr. wrote to his mother after being accepted into the Navy. Being 20 at the time (old enough to be drafted but not old enough to sign up), the Navy required the written pemission of his mother.
(Written and postmarked October 12, 1942)

Frank Long with Mary Lou and George Jr. (1943)

George Jr. in V-12 uniform with George Sr. (1947)

Mabel Rominger (1908)

Charlie Kramer (circa 1928)

Jean and Mary Lou Sayles (1934)

Mary Lou Sayles (1936)

Mary Lou & George at Christmas dance (1944)

All of Mae's kids - Betty, Carolyn, Mary and George Jr. (1947)

George Newton Cahill Sr. (1947)

George Jr. & Mary Lou with Frank Long and Mary Hiloski (1947)

George and Mary Lou's wedding (June 13, 1948)

Mabel and Mae at Mary Lou and George's wedding (1948)

Best man Frank and maid of honor Margaret with newlyweds
Mr. and Mrs. George and Mary Lou Cahill (June 13, 1948)

Mary Lou with her beloved Aunt Helen (Atlanta 1948)

A pregnant Mary Lou wearing the coat given her by Aunt
Helen while George aims his trusty 8mm camera (1958)

Lois Fialco, the "Best baby sitter in the world"
with the six Cahill children (Cleveland 1959)

George and Mary Lou about to move to Canada (1960)

A Sunday with the kids at Stanley Park (Vancouver 1962)

Mary Lou bids farewell as George is about to take his first trip ever to Italy (January 1966)

George and Mary Lou's eight children (Pottsville 1964)

So many summers spent in Florida visiting family
and soaking up the sun (Indian Rocks Beach 1973)

George and Mary Lou celebrate retirement (1986)

Ever devoted sister and brother, Mary Lou and Jean (2001)

If a moment was beautiful, she couldn't help but preserve it, as evidenced by this photo snapped by Mary Lou at Jean's funeral with his wife Dorothy and daughter Liz.

Mary Lou's 80th birthday surrounded by a loving family (2009)

George with his brother Larry and sister Sandy (2009)

Mary Lou and George during one of their last trips abroad.

George N. Cahill at home in his beloved Florida (2022)